10 YEARS SOBER

TAKING STEPS TOWARD FREEDOM

LANCE LANG

LANCE LANG

10 YEARS SOBER

TAKING STEPS
TOWARD FREEDOM

ALLY,

Thank you for loving me

every step of the way.

RIDE OR DIE.

❤

A WORD BEFORE...

As I write this, it is Day 3000-something of my sobriety, and it is such a different feeling than Day One was. Even though that first day was almost ten years ago, I still remember it like it was yesterday. I look back on who I was then, and I can't believe that man has turned into who I am today. I just wanted to get clean; my vision for myself in ten years from then was so limited. God has brought me so much further than I'd ever imagined.

And yet, when I look at who I am now, none of it is surprising. This is the way it is when you walk with Jesus: He takes you farther into Himself than you ever thought you'd go, all while you realize that this version of you has been struggling to get out all your life. It just takes steps. And if there is a key, outside of Jesus, to any of my success story, it is this: I got to Day 3000-something one step at a time.

There's not a doubt in my mind that I was specifically and

purposefully created to do exactly what I do today. Like me, many residents of the program and their family members get to live out their calling each and every day through a organization I started called Hope is Alive (HIA). HIA exists to radically change the lives of drug addicts, alcoholics, and those who love them. We provide faith-focused mentoring homes for addicted individuals who are transitioning back into the "real world" from treatment centers, correctional facilities, and poor life choices. As I write this, we have over 20 homes and an 89% success rate for all graduates.

Hope is Alive has been blessed to help change thousands of lives, altering the course of hundreds of families for generations to come. Parents getting their children back, men and women finding their career path, bound souls discovering financial freedom, spiritual freedom, emotional freedom... just FREEDOM, period. Always taking steps toward new and better kinds of freedom. Our graduates leave the program equipped emotionally, professionally, spiritually, and financially, along with a toolkit of life skills that enable them to contribute mightily to their respective communities.

Hope is Alive has become known, not just in Oklahoma but

slowly across the country, as the leading voice in addiction recovery programs. There's no one doing it like we're doing it. I don't believe there's anyone seeing the results that we're seeing either.

To God be the glory, great things He has done...and is still doing!

My life today is filled with opportunities: meetings, speaking events, partnerships with some of the largest faith-based organizations and recovery institutions across the nation. Every single week I meet with pastors and leaders, donors and supporters, CEO's and judges, volunteers and those in recovery. My life today is amazing! I have an incredible wife who loves me, supports me, and has been with me since before April 27th, 2011. I live in a beautiful home and lead a beautiful life. My life today is free, and easier than it ever was when I was living in my addiction. I wake up and live the life I never allowed myself to dream of.

What you'll find in these pages is a summation of what I've learned over the last ten years of my sobriety, about myself, about our residents, about running a non-profit, and, most importantly, about the God who loves me exponentially more than I could ever love myself—and who never, not for a moment, gave up on me.

I've learned a lot of life-changing truth over this past decade. My life now is not perfect, but it's purposeful. And it's a whole lot different than where I was on Day One.

PICK UP YOUR MAT

Let me set the stage for the moment of my radical transformation. I was living all by myself, having pushed everyone away. My girlfriend Ally had finally moved on. Friends had given up on me. And I was guzzling upwards of 50 pills a day. I was so hooked on opiates, I would roll over in the middle of the night and take a handful of pills so I could go back to sleep. My body was not my own; it was simply a vessel that kept itself functioning solely so it could seek out its next fix.

I didn't get here overnight; this level of addiction takes time, a decade in my case. The last couple of years were absolutely brutal. I had a morning routine to get myself to a place where I could even go to work. Once there, it was Red Bull and vodka at 9:30am, maybe three or four lines of Oxy off my desk, a handful of Lortabs. that got me where I could work for a couple hours. Then that would start wearing off around 11:30 and my mind would start racing about when I was going to do my next round. I had to start working on getting another batch, setting up pickups with my dealer, sometimes leaving in the middle of the work day, to drive all the way across Oklahoma to meet my dealer. Or it was more Oxy off the desk, another handful of Lortabs to make it to the rest of the day. Then come home, do all that a couple more times, nod off through a Netflix documentary or two. And that was my cycle, on a good day that is.

On a bad day, my addiction led me to breaking into co-workers' homes, stealing money from everyone I knew, pawning jewelry, robbing my grandparents, and countless other despicable and embarrassing acts. All just to stay medicated.

I was completely enslaved. I was pathetic and sad and lonely and physically a wreck. And this had drug on (literally) for years. Leading up to April 6th, 2011, when my uncle knocked on my office door, dragged me into his office and finally told me who I had become. And I don't know that I had recognized from the outside looking in, who I really was to the world. So, he took the liberty to tell me.

"You are a liar," he said. "You're a cheater. Everyone here hates you. I know you're doing illegal things; your family is worried sick. You're a wreck, and if you don't get a plan, if you don't tell me what's going on, then this is over."

I'd been confronted before, whether it was from my parents, or Ally or even her family. And I'd been caught stealing, caught lying, caught doing all kinds of crazy things to get high. But what I'd never done until that moment was truly confessed.

That was the day I finally stopped running. April 6th, 2011.

I was scared, scared of withdrawals. Scared of what my body would do if I stopped. I had no concept of sobriety, had hardly even heard the word and certainly had no idea what it meant. I had resigned myself to believing and thinking that I was going to take pills every day for the rest of my life. And somewhere in my twisted mind, I thought I actually could!

I was lonely. I was depressed. But more than anything, I was deceived.

Thankfully on that day, I could finally see it.

I was so sick and tired of running, and with my back up against the wall, I was able to finally utter the first few words of confession and admit what I was doing, but more importantly, who I'd become.

"I'm hooked and I don't know what to do," I said. "I'm scared. I'm really, really scared."

I started crying. My uncle didn't know what to do with me, but Jesus did. And in that moment, something clicked, and I slowly, ever so slightly, I began to change.

I do believe that confession began to loosen the chains of bondage I was in. Something happened inside me in that moment and I had my first inkling of surrender—something I would learn steadily over the next ten years. All the walls I'd built up, all the excuses I'd yelled to drown out the truth about myself—it all started to crumble. For years I was the king of half-truths, but that day I laid it all out for the very first time.

I felt naked, honestly. And that kind of vulnerability was terrifying.

Someone knew the depths of my despair.

And they helped me do something about it.

My uncle got me help, and I went into detox center just days later.

I'll never forget being in detox Easter Day in 2011. My parents are pastors, so Easter is obviously the biggest day of the year for them. It is the biggest day of celebration in Christendom. "Up from the grave He arose." And after leading church services all day that Sunday, they had to go see their son in a pretty rough environment, in a state-funded detox facility in Oklahoma City, decked out in medical scrubs and full of medication.

Over ten days I was slowly weaned off the drugs and alcohol, smoking cigarettes and just trying to try to stay alive. But my mind was racing in its old cycles. I tried to convince the people around me, the doctors and staff that I was okay, that I'd be fine after the detox and didn't need to go anywhere else.

I got out a day early and convinced my parents I was okay to go back to my house for one more night before going to a treatment center. As I sat in the passenger seat of my dad's car, I began convincing him of how good I felt and how I could stay by myself for one more night, all while holding my phone in my right hand out of sight and frantically texting my dealer, who wasn't getting back to me!

I also had nothing. No cash, nothing in my bank account. All my credit cards were maxed out. No gas in my car. I was planning on rifling through my car for loose change and rummaging through every pocket and every piece of clothing I owned to see if there was any money or, better yet, pills anywhere.

I spent the night pacing around, withdrawing from the detox drugs they'd given me, chain-smoking cigarettes just to give my very confused body something to do. I also texted and called my dealer over and over.

No response.

It was one of the longest, loneliest nights of my life.

But it ended in surrender. The next morning, exhausted, still withdrawing, eyes blood shot and body beaten....I took the step. I went to treatment.

And that began Day One.

My parents drove me to the treatment center that morning. We snaked up the long road that led to the center's entrance and parked, and that was the moment when my phone buzzed. Surprise, surprise it was my dealer, finally calling me back.

What was I going to do now, in the cold light of day, standing on the edge of radical life change? Would I take the call I so desperately wanted to get the night before? Could I find a way to manipulate my way out of going to this facility, hitchhike it back to my house, steal some money from a neighbor, pawn some jewelry, risk my freedom, just to meet my dealer ONE LAST TIME?! Is it worth it? Could I get away with it?

About the time this crazy string of thoughts was beginning to make some sense to my insane brain, it hit me: God had been protecting me from myself all night long. God was for me. God was with me. God wanted more for me than I even wanted for myself.

With a flood of love overwhelming my heart and fear rushing through my mind, I got out of the car and went inside.

Thank God, I never answered the phone.

SMOKE PITS & GROUP SESSIONS

One of the first things I remember about treatment is going to the smoke pit. Every treatment center has a good smoke pit where you can smoke a cigarette and just talk with people or think a relaxing thought for a moment.

So there I was, listening to the guys there talking, telling their stories, and it hits me for the first time ever: these dudes are a lot like me. They looked like me. They felt like me. They told stories like me. They had done bad stuff like me. They'd got caught like me. They were here... with me!

My addiction was mine alone, but in that smoke pit on that first day in treatment, I realized for the first time that *I wasn't alone.* It was the first time I felt the embrace of a community of people who were commonly afflicted and chasing the same goals.

I went back to my room and my exhausted body finally gave

up after its previous sleepless night of stress. I passed out on the bed and knew nothing until a knock on the door. My counselor had brazenly let himself in.

"Hey, you're late to your first group," he said

"What's a group?" I said.

"Group counseling, it's 1:15 and it's time for your group therapy session."

I sprang out of bed, apologizing. It was the first moments of my first day of sobriety, and I was clueless. I threw on some clean clothes and apologized all the way down the hallway and into the first group session.

Here were these guys I'd just met out in the smoke pit, and now they're sitting in a circle. I looked across, took inventory, and found a seat.

"Well, men, we've got a new guy here today," said the counselor. "His name is Lance."

I felt their eyes on me. I felt seen.

"Lance," the counselor said, "tell us your story."

I didn't know what I was doing. I didn't know what would happen from that moment forward. All I knew was that it was time to tell my story.

SAYING YES, AGAIN AND AGAIN

Each day between Day One and Day 3000-Something has been an incredible blessing. Since that first therapy session, I've told my story probably close to 1200 times, in just about every environment you can imagine: treatment centers, group sessions, church services filled with folks dressed in their Sunday best, church services filled with recently released inmates, on the streets to the unhoused and in multi-million-dollar homes to business executives.

Stories connect us to others. The stories of our lives are our secret weapons, and I'm always looking for reasons to use mine.

The story of recovery always starts with a willingness to say *yes* to whatever God asks you to do in those first few months of treatment. No matter how crazy that *yes* might seem to you.

I think of the story in the gospels where Jesus encounters a paralyzed man and first forgives his sin. All the religious leaders freak out, and so Jesus also heals the man, saying to him, "Stand up, take up your mat, and walk home."

And the man does it! He stands up, picks up his mat, and walks home.

I like to think of that man using that mat for the rest of his life, and every time he sat on it, whether at home or on a picnic or at a town meeting, he used it as a way to tell his story. "See this mat?" he'd say. "An interesting thing about it…"

With that simple mat, with his story, he could change the world.

During my first year of sobriety, I didn't think I was going to change the world, necessarily, but I knew that I had a call on my life. Praying on my knees, next to my bunk in room number nine, halfway through my stint in rehab, I believe God called me to use my story to make an impact in this world. And I knew that my response from that moment forward had to be *yes*.

I didn't have a choice anymore. I truly felt that I lost my ability to choose, and honestly that that was a blessing. After all, I had chosen selfishly for a decade of my life.

I had chosen to hurt people.

I had chosen to ruin my calling.

I had chosen to put drugs into my system.

I had chosen to impact those who were around me.

I had chosen to be a bad friend.

I had chosen to be a bad son.

I had chosen these things, but God had chosen to give me a second chance.

I believe the only choice I had was to say *yes* to whatever He asked me to do and wherever He asked me to go.

And so the theme of my first year of sobriety became this: **say *yes*.** Whatever God said to do? *Yes.* I saw myself in that man who was healed, who got up, who took his mat, who used that mat to tell his story.

And of course you know what happened: God began to give me those opportunities, it seemed immediate. About two weeks into my stay, our regular Thursday-night Bible study leader was a no-show, so the director of the facility turned to me.

"Lance, your dad is a pastor," he said. "Would you mind leading the Bible study tonight?"

This is exactly what I had dealt with my entire life: somebody stereotyping me because I was a pastor's kid to do something publicly spiritual, like pray before the meal or just talk about the Bible off the top of my head. This is all I had been running from! But in that moment I knew my answer had to be *yes* and so even though I was nervous and scared to get in front of my peers, at a facility where I was trying to get my life back, I still said ***yes.***

I guess I did fine, because the facility asked me to start leading a Bible study every morning at 10:15. I didn't know who would show up, but I told the guys what I was doing. That first day it was just me and one other guy. The next day there were three of us. And the more I said *yes*, the more it began to grow, and the more confidence I got to keep saying *yes* when I got out.

After my time at the treatment center was up, they asked me to go to a sober living house. My answer, **Yes**. Pretty soon after that my dad asked me to tell my story at his church. My answer, **Yes**

About three months after I was out of treatment, the owner of the center asked me to consider working there, to actually become the Executive Director with only six months of sobriety. Even though I was set up in a great family business (with a great future ahead) and even though this was a crazy thing to ask someone with six months clean: I still said **Yes!**

Yes after *yes* after **yes**.

When we say *yes,* we get an ongoing glimpse of what God does on the other side of that *yes*, proving his faithfulness as we grow in our obedience and further allowing us to internalize the truth that the best is yet to come.

Telling you to say *yes* is a nice, inspirational, challenging, motivational thing to say. And I do truly believe God loves to see us take steps of obedience. That there is incredible growth, reward, and blessings when we put ourselves in uncomfortable situations.

But you also have to know that there's discomfort on that other side. That's one of the incredible blessings of sobriety, especially in that first year: discovering that growth comes in the uncomfortable places. As I like to say: no challenge, no change.

Saying *yes* is challenging, but it produces change, every single time.

I had to prepare for a dozens of new opportunities to speak or to tell my story in that first year, or take that new job. Or really make any step in a different direction, which is really the entire first year of your sobriety. In a sense, it's teaching yourself how to walk again, always stepping out into uncomfortable places and putting yourself in uncomfortable positions, like going back to people you've hurt or places where you've been embarrassed and making amends.

I remember going back to my old job and facing all my

coworkers to apologize publicly the first Monday I was back. That took preparation. It took time and mental stimulation. That was tough. But I had to say *yes* to it.

You have to realize that every time you say *yes*, you will feel uncomfortable, every time. But that feeling of anxiety, that's what growth, feels like. Even though you rarely see the growth in the moment, it's happening. It's like when you were a kid and your parents measured your height against a wall, or maybe a door jamb. You don't ever really feel yourself growing—you only know you grew because you can see the marks on the wall getting higher and higher each time you turn around.

I can look back at my journey of sobriety, and I can tell that the first year I grew exponentially, and it's because God challenged me to change, to say *yes*.

A MIRACLE IN MOTION

Let's take a closer look at the story of the paralyzed man as it's found in Luke 5:17-26, because I think there are a few key things we can learn here.

First, the posture in which we come to the Healer is important. The man didn't bellow a demand; he humbled himself and was literally lowered before Jesus. When you want to be healed, you must first become humble.

Notice also how there is a lot of different characters in the story. I've been each of these characters before (well, except for Jesus). You may see yourself as the paralyzed man, or you may see yourself as the friends who are taking him to see Jesus. Or, perhaps you've been the crowd of religious people who were so concerned about their interpretation of right and wrong that they almost missed a miracle. I know I've been that guy *for sure*. Which one are you today? Which one do you wish to be?

Oh, and maybe my favorite part about this story is the way it ends. This is too good for me to paraphrase:

"Immediately he stood up in front of them, took what he had been lying on, and went home praising God. Everyone was amazed and gave praise to God. They were filled with awe and said, 'We have seen remarkable things today.'"

He got up immediately, and his first reaction was praise. And that's what he did, all the way home.

He put his miracle into motion. And it made people take notice, not of him, but of the power of Jesus.

That's my hope for my story. That you see the miracle God

did in my life and recognize the miracle He's doing in yours. Just like this man, you can be a miracle in motion.

You already *are* a miracle.

If you're drawing breath, you are a miracle.

If you were once lost, but now are found, you are a miracle.

If you were once blind, but now you can see, you are a miracle.

If you have overcome addiction, you are a miracle.

If you have walked through a divorce, or sexual abuse, or a generational   curse you are a miracle.

Are you alive, on this planet, right this second? You're a miracle.

Do you dare to say it to yourself?

"I am a miracle!"

Go ahead, give it a try.

"I am a miracle!"

Now this time outloud, with some passion... "I am a miracle!"

Good job!

Now, maybe you don't feel like a miracle. The good thing is: it doesn't matter whether you feel like it or not! No matter what has happened to you, you always have another chance! That makes you a miracle.

Some people may call you an anomaly, an oddity, or an abnormality, but God calls you a miracle!

You might not see it today.

You might not remember when it happened.

You might not appreciate it.

You might not have even wanted it.

Too bad! You're still a miracle.

Are you brave enough to believe it?

Thinking of our story, another thing that strikes me is the necessity in the story of this man's friends. God can do a miracle anytime He wants, but Jesus waits until this man's friends put him in a position to be healed. It took others to get him to the place where he was ready to receive the miracle. Jesus loves to let other people play party to His miracles. We rarely receive miracles without the help of someone else.

Which leads to another question: are you the kind of person who always needs healing, or are you the kind of person who also takes people to the Healer?

This man's friends loved him so much they risked ridicule, injury, and a very upset homeowner to get him in front of Jesus.

You've probably had people in your life like this, people who've carried you, who've torn the roof off the place on your behalf.

The great thing is that *you* can be someone like that for *someone else*. My uncle, my parents and Ally were all those people for me, calling me out on my addiction and loving me enough to get me in front of Jesus in that treatment center. I hope I've repaid them by becoming someone who takes other people to the Healer.

The cool thing is that when you become a friend like that, you still get to participate in the miracle. Check out verse 20, which says, "When Jesus saw *their* faith, he said, "Friend, your sins are forgiven.""

It wasn't just the man's faith alone—it was *their* faith, collectively, that put the miracle into motion.

Another thing to notice about this passage is that it doesn't say their faith made his legs start working. No, it tells us their faith was the thing Jesus saw to forgive the man's sins, heal his heart, and set him right internally in his spirit. And then, as icing on the cake (and to shut up the religious folks), Jesus healed the man.

This is important: God will always change a heart before He

changes the affliction. The heart must be made new, which is why Jesus forgave the sins, then He healed the legs. If you're wondering why you can't break the curse of your hands, your eyes, or your addiction, maybe it's because you haven't first accepted the forgiveness of your heart.

Okay, let's change gears. Put yourself in the position of the paralyzed man. You have been crippled your entire life, and your friends drop you in front of Jesus, who looks to you and says, because of those friends He forgives you. Then He tells you to get up, take your mat, and go home.

Do you believe Him? You might as well. So, you try to stand to your feet *for the first time in your life*! And you begin to feel the strength in your legs, and you can't believe it but at the same time, it is the easiest thing to believe.

You pick up that mat and you run home, praising God the whole way. You tell the story over and over and over again, showing people the dirty, filthy mat that you sat on for years and years. But how in a moment, God wrapped in flesh looked at you and said Get up! Your sins are forgiven your affliction has been healed now go, go, take your mat and be a miracle in motion.

That mat represents your past. For me, that mat was my addiction. I was stuck on it, no matter how gross, how filthy it got. Shameful, humiliating, embarrassing... couldn't get off it. But Jesus healed me, and now I can carry that mat—the past, as told in my story—and I can show it to other people. I don't live on it anymore; it lives to serve God.

What's your mat? What are you doing with it?

Have you gotten off your mat, picked it up, and decided to be a miracle in motion?

God doesn't save us to be stagnant, and He doesn't save us just for ourselves. God did a miracle in you so that you can now be a part of someone else's miracle. God is purposeful, He is intentional. He has a plan, and it's not for you to sulk around acting sorry for yourself. It's not for you to sit around on top of your "mat" and just let your miracle go to waste.

Are you missing out on what He has because you won't get off your mat? Oftentimes, God heals us or sends a miracle into our lives, but He never wants to see us passively receive that healing or miracle. God wants us to act on it! God wants us to say *yes* by picking up our mats and walking back into the life He called us to live.

I've never once regretted any of the *yeses* I've said to God.

Not for a second. And I can promise you this: you won't either.

So, pick up your mat. Say *yes*. What do you have to lose?

More importantly…what do you have to GAIN?!

YOUR SECRET WEAPON

I celebrated the first anniversary of my sobriety in the same place I started it: at that treatment center, in a group session. Except this time, instead of introducing myself to everyone in the room, everyone already knew who I was.

I was the Executive Director there.

I only had one year of sobriety. Yet, through a series of wild circumstances and relationships, my *yeses* had gotten me to that place.

That first-year celebration was a monumental moment, sitting in that group session, crying tears of gratitude about how thankful I was to get to that one year of sobriety mark and recapping all the things that happened during that first year and all this change that was taking place. Everything my *yes* had enabled.

With this new job as the Director of the very facility I had just gone through 9 months prior, I had begun meeting with community leaders and pastors, telling them about this place, and we were making tremendous inroads. We were raising money, building things, adding new initiatives and getting out the word across the state. I truly thought I found my purpose that I had stepped into the calling God had on my life.

For the first time in my professional life, things felt natural. I would talk to people and the words would just flow from my mouth. People would have really strong responses to things I said or did and would feel deeply impacted. It really felt, for almost the first time in my life, that what I was doing was making a positive difference in the world, and that I had finally embarked on the beginning of the rest of my life.

That feeling of knowing you are doing exactly what you are created to do? There's no other feeling like that in the world. And it's the feeling I felt on June 12, 2012, as I sat in my office and realized no other staff members were there. I began looking around, wondering where everybody was, when I saw the owner pulling into the parking lot. Moments later he took me by surprise when he walked into my office and basically fired me. He was nice about it, but that didn't matter. I was devastated; humiliated. Because not only had that place become a sanctuary for me, but I'd also put everything I knew and loved into it. I'd moved my life down to the small town in Oklahoma where it was located and had done all this work to garner community support and in a matter of literally 20 minutes, everything in my world was put back upside down.

A year of sobriety was a long time, but it wasn't enough to make me super-strong. Even after a year or two of sobriety—or really any length of it—you're still in a very fragile place and tough emotional moments can really flip the whole world on its head. That's what happened to me.

I just moved into a new home on this property, so I had no idea where to go. I was truly homeless. I was lost, devastated, and emotional, so I turned to the one person who had been with me during every step of the journey: Ally.

She was soon right by my side and helped me walk through it, helped me accept what I needed to do for housing: to be a 30-year-old, single, bald, recovering drug addict, who was moving back in with his parents.

Honestly, it was one of the most refreshing and spiritually nurturing times I've ever had in my life. I got to really grow and restore my relationship with my parents. When I had moments of anxiety or embarrassment, my mom would come into my room and read scripture over me. When I dipped into feelings of downright fear over my future, my dad would offer words of reassurance and support. Perhaps it was my own fragility that made this time so sweet, that I got to slow down and have a break at a significant moment. That I got to reset and really sit back and deeply consider: *What do I want to do with my life?*

By saying *yes* my first year sobriety, I'd been given the opportunity to lead some small groups around Oklahoma City, as well as recovery meetings on Wednesday nights. There was a sober living group here in Oklahoma City that allowed me to continue leading groups even though I had been fired from the job that had facilitated them. That, coupled with talking to my dad and praying every night on my knees as to what I was going to do next, began to formulate an idea in my mind and I realized the calling God had given me at that treatment center: to use my story to impact other people.

My calling didn't change when my employment did. And just because things don't work out the way you want them to, doesn't mean the calling God put in your heart is removed either. A true calling never goes away. You just might have to wait, pray and seek a new vehicle in which to carry out the calling God gives you. Just don't give up on the calling, no matter what!

That's what this time at my parents' house gave me. It gave me time to pray for the new vehicle. It gave me space to dream and visualize what my calling would look like in practice. I knew I wanted to work with other men who were early in sobriety, to be able to give some of the blessings I had been given, like mentors and opportunities to grow financially, emotionally, spiritually, and physically. It all began to crystallize, and I realized that I had hope for a dream.

I had the chance to change my life, AGAIN.

HOPE IS ALIVE

Looking back at my time at the treatment center I realized that they were certainly doing decent work, helping people clear the cobwebs in their mind, get their feet back underneath them physically, and probably grow a little bit spiritually, but in that 30-, 60-, 90-day setting, there really wasn't enough time to encourage people to change every facet of their lives.

That's when my hope and dream came into focus, what if we could create a program that touched every single aspect of an individual's life, physically, spiritually, and professionally, restoring their family, building life skills, and all inside the confines of a dynamic community. A community that's focused on growing in their faith, supported by local churches and facilitates opportunities that they would have never had outside of living in a home like this.

So that's what I did.

Later that year, in November 2012, I went to the courthouse and filed the paperwork to create Hope is Alive Ministries.

Sobriety isn't a cure-all for life's struggles. Working a program and changing your life, choosing to say you're going to live of recovery set you up for great success, but it doesn't disqualify you from the pains of life. Instead, it gives you the tools you need to overcome those struggles when they inevitably arise.

I'm really proud to say that even in the midst of this really dramatic situation early in my new life, I was able to make it through clean and sober. The point being—and the aim of this chapter—is that what the enemy meant for evil, God uses for such good.

I really believe that the enemy wanted to take me out. What I thought was the worst thing that could have ever happened in my newfound life of sobriety was actually the best moment ever. God used that moment. I can recall those emotions I felt when I got fired and the world fell out from under me. I was desperate. I was devastated. I truly thought my life was over and my calling was counterfeit, that everything I'd worked for and dreamed of was over in a snap, ripped from my hands. The despair I felt was unimaginable, and I never wanted to feel that way again.

I believe that if you've gone through a tough situation, then you have a story to tell. But I also believe that we have an enemy who does not want us to tell that story. And we might come up against the gates of hell, and it might look like, you know, something that is perceived to be good on the outside but they're trying to slow you down or hold you back.

God has used that moment in such an unbelievable way, by gently guiding me to start Hope is Alive, which has gone on to change so many people's lives. What could have turned evil, God used for such a good. The enemy tried to dash my dream and get me to doubt my purpose, but God used that to build a new dream, a new purpose, and a better life.

Maybe you can relate. Maybe you've seen God breathe holy breath onto the embers of a dream in your heart, fanning that into a burning flame of hope in you. Maybe you've endured pain and suffering and come out the other side with a life-changing story. Maybe you've discovered that Hope is Alive in you.

If you're alive, you have a story of victory. It may not look like my story, but who cares: it's not mine, it's yours.

And it's your secret weapon.

YOUR SECRET WEAPON

Everybody needs somebody to champion and believe in them, someone who will go to bat for them. I didn't realize it at the time, but as I stepped out on my own two feet to start Hope is Alive, those are the kind of people I needed. With those kinds of people in my corner, there's no way I would have been able to get this thing off the ground.

The biggest opportunity I had early on in year two, specifically, was telling my story in front of 3000 men at the Rewired men's conference, and I was only there because of people who believed in me. It started with my dad connecting with Keith, the conference director, and telling him that men needed to start talking about addiction, that the mask around this subject needed to be taken off.

Keith agreed to meet with me, so we went to lunch, where he asked me to tell my story. So, I did, and in that moment, Keith believed in me and gave me the opportunity to tell my story on a stage in front of 3000 men.

This is the power of your story.

It was a night I'll never forget, one that was a catalyst for Hope is Alive. For the first time ever, I was overwhelmed with the visual impact of my story as I told it. Being on that stage, in front of so many people, I could see the large-scale reaction of tears, nodding heads, and looks of conviction as my story unfolded. When I was finished, I witnessed the large-scale power of God as men responded by walking to the altar, taking their literal first steps toward freedom.

This night didn't just give me an opportunity to spread the word about God and what he was beginning to do with Hope is Alive—it gave me a confidence and confirmation that this wasn't just my story—it was God's story, too! And he wanted to use it in a big way.

Stories are sticky. Stories connect people. Stories are how we learn empathy and how we gain inroads not just into the lives of others but also ourselves. When we hear others' stories, we hear echoes of our own. We find common ground.

Studies are coming out of Princeton University demonstrating that the brain waves of people listening to stories actually start to synchronize with those of the storyteller.

For example, say you're experiencing a story that is extremely intense, like the other night when I watched the Oscar-winning documentary *Free Solo*, which documents free climber Alex Honnold attempting to scale a sheer cliff with no safety harness. My palms were sweating, my heart was racing, my eyebrows were arched all the way to the ceiling, and every muscle in my body was tensed as Alex slowly, methodically, made his way up that cliff face.

You've been there. We've all been there. These reactions we have to stories? These are proven by science, letting us know that our stories are powerful.

And that makes your story your secret weapon, but instead of bringing destruction, this weapon can truly inspire and motivate change in other people's lives from the inside out. Stories change people.

Of course, it's nice to have science back us up, but we don't really need to hear it from a laboratory—we already knew this because our Savior taught us this! We've already learned from our Master that stories are a secret weapon God graced us with, because Jesus used them to teach us. Except we don't call them *stories*, we call them *parables*.

Jesus used parables in so many situations, especially when he was trying to get his point across to a crowd, and he almost always started with this phrase: "The kingdom of heaven is like a..."

The kingdom of heaven is like a landowner...

The kingdom of heaven is like a man who sowed good seed in his field...

The kingdom of heaven is like a king who gave a wedding feast for his son...

Why did Jesus engage with his audiences like this? And when we read these stories, what happens? When Jesus uses parables, he's doing many things:

- Taking us on a journey, helping us to visualize and connect with the truth he is telling.
- Engaging our emotions.
- Speaking truth.
- Connecting with us so that we might be changed from

the inside out.

And the same things happen in other people when you use your secret weapon. But just like any weapon, you have to pull this one from your holster and engage it. That's why saying *yes* is so important—you're opening yourself up to God-given opportunities to pull the trigger and tell your story.

I believe if we were really real with ourselves, we would all say we want to live a life that makes a difference. We see others making an impact and deep down inside, we desire to do the same, but we don't know how. It looks impossible.

But when you engage your secret weapon, things that once seemed impossible instantly become possible.

We can often forget that God has called us *coworkers*, that we are working alongside Him to build His kingdom, and that the same power that raised Jesus from the dead lives in us. When you feel that tug on your spirit to engage someone with your story, to lend a helping hand, to bring a meal, to volunteer your time, to give a dollar to someone on the street, that is God saying to you, "Join me! Help me! Use what I have given you! Engage your secret weapon!"

Friends, I know we are fighting a battle, but the good news is we are not fighting unarmed. We have the secret weapon!

God has given us a tool, an instrument to beat down the dark forces of this world. We read in Revelation 12:11 that we overcome by the blood of the lamb and the word of our testimony. When we face the accuser, the lies, the fear, the bondage of sin—we can cram all that stuff in the garbage with our secret weapon: our story.

Don't let the enemy talk you out of the power that your testimony holds.

He will...

...tell you that your story isn't powerful.

...push you to compare your story to someone else's, always unfavorably.

...whisper that you're a fake

...try to convince you that no one needs to hear what you have to say.

How do I know, because I've been there, done that. He's tried to tell me that my story was just another drug-addict-turned-sober story, that it isn't as wild and crazy as others, or that it's not comparable to *that other person's* story.

But I reject that. My story is powerful only because it's God's story of the gospel in my life. I know I'm free, and no one can take that story away from me.

And because of this freedom, God gave me a vision for a place where other addicts could seek a life radically different from anything they would have ever experienced. It would be a place of healing and a house of hope. A place where their relationships would be mended and their finances restored, where they would have mentors passing on life skills and churches circling up around them.

And because I kept telling my story, and the story of this vision, we soon gathered our first five men and opened our first home, where we kept telling stories. Now it wasn't just me with a secret weapon—there were five of us. We were all deploying our weapon as often as we could.

God began to bless it, and one home quickly became two, then three, then four, and so on.

But we are nothing special. We are just people who said *yes* to engaging our secret weapon. God can do the same through you. He really wants to use you to help his hurting children take their own steps toward freedom.

You see there is hope in our secret weapon. And you never

know how your story will impact others. But you have to use it.

I know our pasts can be full of emotions and memories that are painful. But sometimes the hope you need to heal is on the other side of saying *yes* to sharing your God-story.

See, the one place the enemy wants you to live is in the defeat of your past, while God wants you to live in the victory He's given you over that very past. He desires for you to stand firm on that new foundation He has given you. Each time you share your story; you are strengthening that foundation and honing your secret weapon.

Because if you have had an encounter with Jesus and He has changed your life, then you have a secret weapon. It's not complicated, it's not some long process, and God's not waiting to use you until you've got everything fixed in your life. No, God wants to use you *right now.*

The secret weapon God has given you is your story, and the most amazing part is: *no one else has your story.*

You have a secret weapon that is yours and yours alone. It's special and unique, and yet at the same time, it's *exactly what someone needs to hear!*

How does that work? Only in God's economy can your

struggles become someone else's strength. What brought you down can help build up someone else, and what almost defeated you, God can use to help someone else overcome!

God doesn't waste anything. Every past moment, every point of pain, every setback, every downturn is just another chapter heading in the story of God's amazing grace in your life. And each one perfectly qualifies you to speak hope into someone else's pitfalls, strength into someone who shares the same struggles.

So, turn around, have eyes to see those who need what you have to give. It's your secret weapon, but it should never be your secret.

GO DEEPER

Year three was a pivotal year for my sobriety, and for my spiritual development. Those first couple of years, in addition to running Hope is Alive, I was working several other part-time consulting jobs to earn a living. After all, it takes a while to get a non-profit off the ground as you prove yourself through results and start gaining credibility in the community.

During my second year of sobriety, I began to see that this thing could have some momentum. I had the best of both worlds: I was making decent money through side jobs while living in the HIA homes and getting my cup filled in recovery working with men. But although I'd said *yes* to God, I didn't feel like I'd gone all in.

One afternoon I was wrapping up some consulting work—and not work that was just going to help some rich guy get richer; this was an app to help build up the faith-based community through social media. It was rewarding work, and I was getting paid way more than I deserved. I was living comfortable.

And that's when God punctured it all by speaking very clearly: *I didn't call you to be comfortable.*

Side note while you sit with that: this is a great lesson for those of us who are trying to live out our calling. It takes years of sacrifice, or what my dad calls your "earning years." Use that grace.

Anyway, when God said that to me, I knew in my heart He was telling me: this is the journey you're going to go on and you've got to give it everything you have. The Big Book says "half measures avail us nothing," and although that is speaking specifically toward men and women trying to stay sober, I felt as if it pertained to me as well when it came to starting Hope is Alive.

I had to go all in.

So, a month later, I contacted every company for which I had been consulting and I quit. I made a decision that I was going to give this calling—Hope is Alive—everything I had, every spare moment of my life. With God's help, it would be something by which I could not only earn a living but also give my life to.

That was really the theme of year three: I didn't call you to be comfortable. At that point we had one home and five guys; before the end of that year we'd opened two more homes and welcome twenty more men into them. Our method became reproducible and I believe God was in it. Treatment centers, individuals, and counselors began to call and ask us about the program. Word began to get out and the big momentum began to roll. We were done playing in the comfortable shallows and were ready to launch out into the deep.

INTO THE DEEP

Speaking of, let's take a look at one of my favorite gospel passages, found in the fifth chapter of Luke. To set the scene, we have Jesus preaching to a crowd of people who were desperate for a word. He was standing by a lake, and they were just all up in his business trying to hear his life-giving teaching.

Jesus, being a smart and compassionate man who was *always* about His Father's business, spied a couple of boats there next to the lake. They were fishermen's boats, but those guys were done working for the day, probably grumbling as they washed their nets over their pitiful haul from the night before.

No matter. Jesus helped himself into Simon's boat and asked him to launch out a way so He could teach the people in a way they could hear Him. And I guess James and John went out on the other boat, too, because they come into the story. Okay, so: Jesus and these three guys are out on the shallow part of the lake in a couple of boats. And that's where our passage picks up:

When [Jesus] had stopped speaking, He said to Simon, "Launch out into the deep and let down your nets for a catch."

But Simon answered and said to Him, "Master, we have toiled all night and caught nothing; nevertheless, at Your word I will let down the net." And when they had done this, they caught a great number of fish, and their net was breaking. So they signaled to their partners in the other boat to come and help them. And they came and filled both the boats, so that they began to sink.

When Simon Peter saw it, he fell down at Jesus' knees, saying, "Depart from me, for I am a sinful man, O Lord!"

For he and all who were with him were astonished at the catch of fish which they had taken; and so also were James and John, the sons of Zebedee, who were partners with Simon. And Jesus said to Simon, "Do not be afraid. From now on you will catch men." So when they had brought their boats to land, they forsook all and followed Him. (Luke 5:4-11)

I love this passage because while it provides many layers of fruitful thought, it offers a simple message: God is always calling us to go deeper: deeper in prayer, deeper in dependence, deeper in faith, in generosity, in boldness.

Jesus asks us to launch out into the deep because spiritual leadership will never thrive in the shallow. A life going deeper with Jesus requires courage, vulnerability, confession, repentance and dedication to living in a community.

But the reward is worth it.

I love people who cast vision, maybe because I consider myself a vision-caster. I believe God has given me a special gift to see and feel what moments could look like, what people need or want. But the greatest moment of vision-casting we have ever witnessed is right here in this passage.

Jesus starts with one of the simplest, yet most life-changing phrases ever:

"Launch out into the deep and let down your nets for a catch."

Simon, James, and John didn't know it yet, but Jesus knew these guys weren't just hungry for a catch; they were also spiritually hungry. They were thinking of food for themselves, their families, and their community. But Jesus was thinking along completely different lines. He was thinking about faith.

And you know what? They aren't the only ones who have their focus on the wrong kind of hunger. *Everyone* is hungry for a catch. We crave accomplishment, purpose, and love from our families.

From moment one of this encounter, Jesus doesn't mess around. Jesus is like, "I am not here to play games." He just turns straight to Simon and, face to face, basically says, "The time for playing it safe is over. If you really want what I can give you, then you'd better launch in the *deep* waters, buddy."

Jesus was saying: I know where your purpose is, I know where your freedom is, I know what can satisfy you, and it's in the deep waters. Take that step. Launch out. Go DEEPER!

Simon responded as many of us would respond in a similar situation: with a faith crisis. We find what I like to call the "Frank

Sinatra" response in verse 5:

"But Simon answered and said to Him, 'Master, we have toiled all night and caught nothing; nevertheless at Your word I will let down the net.'"

But God, I've been doing it *my way* for so long.

I don't know about you, but I can relate. For years I felt God calling me *to* something, to take my life in a certain direction, but I kept choosing to go my own way. From an early age I felt called to help others, but every chance God gave me to launch out into the deep waters, I followed my own ideas and stayed in the shallows with a whole lot of nothing. This led me to my addiction.

It was only when I decided to trust Jesus in the deep end that I began to see the radical life change that has empowered me through the past ten years.

Before, I was a lot like Simon in this passage: I'd been fishing all night and had nothing to show for it. No catch, no conquering, no victories. I felt like Simon's nets: empty.

Simon had been fishing in the places and spaces that he thought were best suited for a catch. He'd done what he'd always done: hung out at night in the shallow waters, but it was all for nothing.

You aren't going to get anything staying in the dark, safe places. Why? Because you've been called *out of darkness*, rescued from the pit of hell, saved to save others...

That's your calling. What are you doing with it? Are you sitting on the sidelines? Are you too busy being stuck in the problem to even see how powerful you really can be? Are you gossiping about others, acting like you are better than them or spending unnecessary brainpower worrying about what other people think? Are you comparing yourself to others? ... QUIT!!

Quit it! You aren't someone else. *You are you for a reason!* And it's time to launch out into the deep, to go wherever God sends you.

Another thing I love about this story is that when Jesus told them to cast their nets into the deep water, He didn't mean for them to use anything they didn't already have. No rods and reels or heavy-gauge fishing line, no special radar or fish lasers or anything. Nope, it was just the nets they already had in the boat they were already in.

The nets they were washing and mending in verse two. The ones they'd been using for God-knows-how-long; the ones that hadn't secured a thing just a few hours earlier. Those were the tools Jesus gave them.

God has already gifted you with all you need to be the person He has called you to be! Your experiences, skills, talents, hurt, habits, hang-ups, pains, shame, failures, and victories—all these work together for good!

That doesn't mean that you never need to work on growth, or on learning new things, or on gaining new skills. What it means is simply this: you are *already equipped* to start fulfilling God's calling on your life. You don't have to wait for some special sign or for your three-month training regimen to be over. Like Pastor Mike Todd says, "All you have, is all you need!" So, get out there into the deep waters with what you have! Lead with what God's already given you.

You don't need anything other than Jesus to bring in a huge catch.

Jesus + nothing = everything.

We find the fulfillment of a life lived out in the deep, on the edge of faith, in verses 6 and 7:

"And when they had done this, they caught a great number of fish, and their net was breaking. So, they signaled to their partners in the other boat to come and help them. And they came and filled both the boats, so that they began to sink."

The night before Jesus appeared, Simon, James, and John had been fishing in their own personal strength...that had resulted in nothing. But when Jesus showed up, suddenly the boat overflowed.

It reminds me of one of my favorite scriptures, found in Ephesians 3:20 (NASB): "Now to him who is able to do far more abundantly beyond all that we could ask or think, according to the power that works within us."

That power working within us? That's the Holy Spirit. With Jesus guiding you and the Holy Spirit working within you, you can do anything.

You can relate to your spouse like you've always wanted to do.

You can restore your relationship with your child, or your parents.

You can step out and start the business God has called you to start.

You can find the courage to say *no* to the things that have torn you apart.

You can go where God wants you to go.

You can live the life He's calling you to live.

Will you say *yes* to what He asks you?

Will you go where He sends you?

Will you lead with what He has given you?

Will you take Jesus and your empty nets out into the deep water? You'll be amazed at what you find out there.

NUNC COEPI

It's year four and now it's time to bounce around a bit as I go deep on my second-greatest love story (after the one between me and God): my amazing wife, Ally.

Ally and I met in mid-March 2008. At the time, I was pretty far into my addiction, although I didn't really realize it. I was smoking weed, taking pills, and drinking a lot. I wasn't full blown, but I was pretty far into it. Ally calls it my "Train Wreck Season".

True story, though: when I first met Ally, I was so just completely smitten, overwhelmed, and in love, that I stopped using any drugs. It wasn't a conscious decision. I was just so infatuated with her. I'd never met anyone like her. She was from somewhere different. She grew up somewhere different. She had gone to college in Arizona, had lived in LA and worked for a famous fashion designer. On top of that, she was beautiful.

And she was willing to talk to me!

The very first time we even talked was at a bar, where we kind of hung out that night and drove around and stayed up late, just kind of talking to each other. Weirdly, I didn't even get her number. Luckily, a girl that worked for me knew her, so that entire next week, I kept going into this girl's office saying, "Hey, you think I could get that girl's number?" It took some boss pressure, but I eventually got the number. Maybe two weeks later I finally got the courage to call her, and we ended up talking for six hours on the phone that very first night!

I've done everything really fast in my life. I don't have a governor; I'm just always at 110%. Ally is much the same way. So, we just fell head over heels and things moved really quickly in our relationship. I mean, we were engaged within six months, were planning a wedding, and things were going great... except my pill addiction just continued to grow, grow, and grow.

Even when I proposed to her I was on a downward slide. I took her to Peru and was way over the top, proposing on the top of Machu Picchu. Right in the middle, underneath a tree you have to illegally jump a fence to reach. It looked great on the outside, but inside I was a mess, literally having to take handfuls of pills just to stay "sane" on the bus ride to the top of Machu

Picchu

Ally began to realize this, even asking me what was going on with me, telling me how I didn't look very healthy. A couple of times I broke down and did what most drug addicts do: told her just enough truth to get by. I told her I had to take some pills for back pain, which she volunteered to hold for me or to administer. But I always said I was strong enough to do it. I would leave to go meet my dealer, and it got to the point where she would just beg me not to go. And it was around that time that our relationship began to go completely sour. Fights in the street ensued about anything and everything. Her family was on to me; they absolutely did not like me at all. With good reason!

My addiction was so out of control that all I did was chase drugs. And all Ally did was chase me. It was a never-ending race, except there was no finish line and no one could catch what was in front of them.

Where did that lead us? It led to me in full-blown addiction willing to do anything I possibly can to whoever it is to get high. It led to her falling in a deep way into codependency and enabling, which destroyed her understanding of our relationship. Rightfully so, she began to open her eyes to what other relationships would look like.

It took a few years, but she finally moved on around Valentine's Day of 2011, about three months before my sobriety began. I lied to her for the last time. I had gone alone to try to find some drugs. She called me and asked where I was, and I told her I was at the Grand Lake Casino in a small town in Oklahoma, thinking I was smart. But she was smarter. She asked me what color the carpet was while searching for pictures of the interior of the casino online. I told her it was blue. The pictures told her it was red. And that was it.

When Ally broke things off with me, my isolation really set in and I just spent time at my house all by myself, completely alone. She would tell you she didn't completely withdraw from my life: there were nights when she would come over and find her way into my house just to check on me, only to find me passed out. She just checked my pulse to make sure I was still alive, and then leave.

ALLY'S CALLING

Okay, so off I go to treatment to get sober and, strangely, Ally and I were still very much part of each other's lives. So much so that when I was in treatment, I mean she actually came down and went through a few sessions with me, with my counselor, because we needed to begin some healing—not even for our relationship, but just for our own health.

Treatment and rehab can often be unfair for the loved ones of addicts. They get all this help, because they've been the one causing all the problems. And yet, their family members are often left holding the bag and dealing with their own trauma. And that's a very good example of what happened to Ally, who had endured a severely traumatic and verbally abusive relationship.

She was in a state of trying to pick up the pieces, even if she didn't quite realize it. Trying to deal with the head and heart level trauma I had left her with, all while I'm getting all the help and growing and becoming happy and hopeful.

Nevertheless, she was there. We talked frequently. She was involved in what I was doing. Even when I was fired from the treatment center, it was her I called to come help pack my stuff. She's always been my rock. She has always been the one that I've leaned on, even if sometimes I had to insert myself in her attempts to move on.

So, for the next three or four years of our lives, I wanted to be back in a relationship with her, but you know, trust takes time. And it took a long time for her to regain trust in me; it took an especially long time for her family to regain trust in me. Which is a great lesson for people who have gone through traumatic issues or infidelity and relationships, addiction, dishonesty, and the like? Rebuilding and regaining trust takes a long time.

She was there every step of the way. The night we released my first book, *Hope is Alive*, Ally was the one who organized the party. When we went and looked for the first Hope House, I wanted her to look at the house to know what she thought about it. When we opened the home and we moved in, Ally was there, giving directions for furniture, decorating like she always has. (side note, she's decorated every HIA house since...)

That is the really cool part about what God did in our restoration story by allowing her to be a part of some of Hope is Alive's first moments. He knew she would be a critical and integral part of the ministry's growth. It's just a reminder that nothing is ever wasted. God will use every bit of the pain and the struggle and all the heartache, all the crazy situations, if we will just allow Him to do so.

FREEDOM TO FALL

One of the incredible blessings of sobriety is that you get the chance to "begin again". Oftentimes this means new starts all over the place: jobs, relationships, careers, hobbies, health, finances... you get the idea.

Part of beginning again means that you are given the chance to reclaim your legacy. And I don't know about you, but where I am in my life, I'm thinking more and more about the legacy I will leave.

Is that something you think about? The big legacy questions like:

- What will people say about me when I'm gone?
- What am I leaving behind?
- How will I be remembered?

Here's the truth: no matter where you are right now, you have the power to leave the legacy that you desire. You hold the pen that writes the story of your life.

But here's the challenge: when you choose to say *yes* to God, you become a target! The enemy is after you! He hates that you have chosen this life and he wants to take you out, so he does all he can to put up roadblocks.

- Family issues

- Financial issues

- Health issues

- Legal issues

Most importantly, the enemy works not just on the things in your hands like money, relationships, or your career, but also on the things in your head. He will tell you over and over again, that who you used to be is who you always are. That your God-chasing life is a façade, that you don't have what it takes to fulfill your calling.

But of course, we know that's a lie! You were born for greatness. You were born to have a legacy of life change!

You can't blend in when you were born to stand out!

The fact is everyone falls down. It's just that not everyone gets back up. Why? Because they're scared to fall again! It makes sense and is a very human response. When I was in the thrall of my addiction, I fell down and stayed down, and then made sure to take enough pills to keep myself down, down, down.

But a legacy comes from a life of taking risks. Like we learned in the last chapter, you have to launch out into the deep. To grow, you've got to stretch; to explore, you've got to pioneer new areas; to discover your limits, and you have to push the boundaries.

No one ever changed the world by playing it safe.

The essence of what we do at Hope is Alive, the culture we are trying to create, is summed up in this single phrase:

We give men and women the freedom to fall and the courage to stand back up again.

It's really that simple

To be a change-maker, world-shaker, and legacy-writer, you've got to give yourself the freedom to fall.

I wouldn't be where I am today if I hadn't given myself this freedom. From running for class vice president as an eighth-grader to taking a job I would eventually lose to founding a non-profit with next-to-no expertise on running one, God has consistently called me to a position where I had the freedom to fall. Sometimes I fell spectacularly; sometimes I only stumbled; sometimes I walked a long way. But when it comes to following God, I've had to put myself out there.

And the same goes for you. You'll never grow into the person you truly desire to be by living a life of comfort.

You might be saying I don't have those opportunities! I'm not being asked to speak at a men's conference or start a non-profit organization. I hear you. Ten years ago, I would've said the same thing. But today, I would tell you *quit lying to yourself.* You have been chosen by God to live a life of legacy. He has not done it by accident, He chose you because He wants to *use* you, and He equips who He chooses. Your experiences are your equipment! Your story is your secret weapon! All you have to do is start listening, open your eyes, and start saying *yes* to the opportunities God puts in front of you!

And once you do, you've got to push yourself beyond *you.* You've got take it to such a limit (launch into the deep!) that something *greater* than you can show up.

You've got to give yourself freedom to fall, because it's in the fall where we learn the lessons, where we realize how much we need others, where we find new strength, where we begin to decipher our gifts and where our callings are clarified. Here are just a few people who have found something greater when they gave themselves the freedom to fall:

Oprah Winfrey was publicly fired from her first television job as an anchor in Baltimore for getting "too emotionally invested in her stories." But she obviously got right back up from that fall to become the undisputed queen of television talk shows before amassing a media empire.

Soichiro Honda's billion-dollar automobile business began with a series of failures and fortunate turns of luck. He was turned down by Toyota Motor Corporation after interviewing for a position as an engineer, leaving him jobless for quite some time. He started making scooters of his own at home, and then, after some encouragement from his neighbors, finally started his own business.

Harland David Sanders is better known as Colonel Sanders of Kentucky Fried Chicken fame, and his now-famous secret chicken recipe was rejected just over a thousand times before a restaurant accepted it.

Walt Disney had a bit of a rough start, fired in his first career by a newspaper editor because, "he lacked imagination and had no good ideas." After that, he started a number of businesses that ended with bankruptcy and failure. We know how it all turned out, obviously.

What do all these people have in common? When they fell, they all got back up again. They learned lessons from their time on the ground, but they never got comfortable down there.

They also all possessed the power of a short memory. By

that, I mean that they shut down the negative internal voice that would tell them they needed to stay fallen. When they experienced rejection after rejection, they didn't let that get into their long-term thinking. Instead, they pressed on, undaunted by their past falls.

Are you allowing your past to predict your present? Quit! You are not who you used to be; today, you are a new creation! You are a miracle in motion! You are a fighter! You are a winner! You are a change-maker! A world-shaker! A legacy-keeper!

But here's the thing about short memories: just as they apply to our falls, they also apply to our successes. We can't fall into the trap of thinking that what we accomplished last week, last month, or last quarter is something we can rest on. Sobriety is a daily pursuit, and so is your calling from God.

This can all be embodied in an attitude that is summed up by the Latin phrase *Nunc Coepi* (and in case you're wondering, it's pronounced "NOONK chay-PEA"). This phrase, taken from a Latin translation of the Psalms, basically means "Now I Begin." It is a forward-facing posture that says, "Okay, I fell, but I've stood back up and now I begin again."

Of all the ingredients necessary to be the man or woman

God has called you to be, this one may be the most important. It's the strength deep inside your gut to get back up again.

When I think about the people in my life who have left a legacy, who have changed something, who have altered the world for those who will fill it when they leave, they all possess this inner strength. This *Nunc Coepi* attitude.

One of my favorite stories in the Bible is about a man named Joseph. Not Jesus' father—the Old Testament one. This Joseph endured many hardships, but got back up and began again each time.

Joseph was one of the youngest of a bunch of brothers, but he was the favorite of his dad, Jacob. Which, of course, made him less-than-popular among his older brothers.

When Joseph was seventeen years old he had two dreams that got so under his brothers' skin that they started plotting ways to get rid of him. In the first dream, Joseph and his brothers gathered bundles of grain—and then his brothers' bundles started bowing down to his bundle. The second dream was even worse: the sun, the moon, and eleven stars—which represented Jacob, Rachel (Joseph's mother), and his eleven brothers—all bowed to Joseph himself.

That was just too much for his brothers. Those dreams caused his brothers to act out in anger and envy, first trying to kill him before selling him into slavery in Egypt.

After being bought and "exported" to Egypt, Joseph found himself in a decent position, but he also found more trouble. An ambitious lady put her eyes on him. After declining her "advances", he was accused sexual harassment, and because the lady's husband was not only the offended partner but also Joseph's boss, judge, and ruler, poor Joe ended up getting undeserved punishment in jail.

But did he quit? Did he give up? Did he stop doing what he was called to do?

Nope. He continued to work hard, staying the course and acting with integrity as the man he was called to be. And because of Joseph's character, the warden put him in charge of the other prisoners.

Soon afterward, Pharaoh's chief cupbearer made Pharaoh mad, which landed him in the clink with Joseph. While there, the cupbearer dreamed a crazy dream and mentioned it to Joseph, who, as we know, had a little experience with dreams. Joseph interpreted the dream and asked the cupbearer to remember him when he was inevitably reinstated. This, surely, would be his ticket out of this unjust confinement.

Except... the cupbearer forgot.

Joseph stayed there *two more years*! Can you imagine that?!

Anyway, Pharaoh eventually dreamed some crazy dreams of his own, and when his advisers failed to interpret them, the cupbearer *finally* remembered Joseph, who was summoned to appear before Pharaoh to interpret his dreams.

Joseph could have said no. He could have maintained a long memory, or hidden in the jail so he was not in a position to fall again. He could've told himself that prison was all he was good for.

But he didn't. He embodied a spirt of *Nunc Coepi.*

He interpreted the dream as a prophecy: The entire area was about to have seven years of abundance followed by seven years of famine. Joseph advised the Pharaoh to store surplus grain so they could handle the famine when it arose.

Pharaoh was so impressed that he hauled Joseph right out of prison for good and made him second-in-command of all of Egypt. All of Joseph's dreams and stories were now vindicated, but he didn't for a second let it go to his head. If you read further into the story, years later Joseph also seizes an incredible opportunity to show forgiveness to those brothers who sold him into slavery to begin with—though only after they bow down to him, fulfilling his dream.

Joseph was called to change the world, but along the way he faced storm after storm, challenge after challenge, and each time he chose to dust himself off. He got up and gave himself freedom to fall, maintained a short memory & he always began again, maintaining that *Nunc Coepi* attitude.

From the first time I heard this phrase it's stuck to my soul, reminding me in just a couple words that I will not be remembered for what I used to do or even what I am doing. I will be remembered for my ability to begin again.

It is because of that ability, the ability to begin again, springs everything else. If I can't learn to *Nunc Coepi* then I am destined to repeat my past, and the same goes for you.

When something hits you, knocks you down, dust yourself off again: *Nunc Coepi*, now I begin.

When you try something new and it doesn't go like you thought it would: *Nunc Coepi*, now I begin.

When a job doesn't see the potential you have inside of you

and they go with someone else, just know God has a better plan and keep pressing on: *Nunc Coepi*, now I begin.

When a relationship ends that you thought might be the one, realize God is saving you from something not beneficial and just keep praying for the right one: *Nunc Coepi*, now I begin.

If you have messed up and you are still stuck in a relapse mindset or a negative frame of mind, make today the day that you start over: *Nunc Coepi*, now I begin.

When you put yourself out there and someone starts hating on you, shake off those ignorant haters and just say to yourself: *Nunc Coepi*, now I begin.

But realize this: you are not alone. You never *Nunc Coepi* on your own, you have the spirit of the living God within you. And that is a powerful, powerful ally. Check out this passage from the Message translation:

"This is what GOD says, the God who builds a road right through the ocean, who carves a path through pounding waves, The God who summons horses and chariots and armies— they lie down and then can't get up; they're snuffed out like so many candles: "Forget about what's

happened; don't keep going over old history. Be alert, be present. I'm about to do something brand-new. It's bursting out! Don't you see it? There it is! I'm making a road through the desert, rivers in the badlands. Wild animals will say 'Thank you!' —the coyotes and the buzzards— Because I provided water in the desert, rivers through the sunbaked earth, Drinking water for the people I chose, the people I made especially for myself, a people custom-made to praise me." (Isaiah 43:16-21)

We fight this world with the strength of a God who builds roads right through the ocean.

We stand and *Nunc Coepi* with a God who carves a path through pounding waves.

And He is always making things new.

So, the next time you think you are done, disqualified, or in despair, choose to remember what God has done in your life, stand back up, and say: *Nunc Coepi*, now I begin!

THE EMAIL THAT CHANGED THE WORLD

Through those first few years, Ally kept me in the friendzone, and rightfully so! But in the summer of 2015, she finally began to realize just how good-looking I was! Nah, just joking! But I do think a lot of things were changing inside her heart. Mainly, she would tell you she began to feel this pull from God on her life to do something in the ministry of Hope is Alive. As she describes it, she would go with me when I preached on Sundays all across churches in Oklahoma; afterward people would come to the table to purchase the books, and a lot of times they would be parents and it was great to be able to tell them where they could send their son.

But then there were those who had a daughter or a wife who needed our program, and we had nothing for them. That was always so tough and challenging. We have no place to send them.

Ally saw that and God began to work on her. She began to realize she was in a cycle of codependency and so she went to treatment for a couple of weeks to work on that. She came out with a much greater understanding of herself, of our relationship and of her role in Hope is Alive. It all led to her writing me an email about starting a women's program and how she felt like God was saying she needed to be involved in the ministry.

Here's a portion of the email Ally wrote me on August 30th, 2015:

My love,

I've been praying very hard and working even harder at listening to God's response regarding the HIA Women's Program. With every prayer I lift up I find myself knowing without a doubt that God has been preparing me for this but even more importantly, our relationship for this.

I've innately known since I was a little girl that God gave me a generous heart. With this immense blessing I've had a stirring to give to others beyond measure, to be of service to others in order to fulfill my calling from God. I've had unease about my calling for years, my chosen path seemed like God was making it hard for me. It all brought me frustration, depression, questioning and even at times unfaithfulness to Him. God opened my eyes to understand each and every one of these unwanted attributes were delivered by Him to keep me pushing and searching for a calling He perfectly created me to fulfill.

As I write this I can't help but know in God's beauty, He has had a plan for us all along and for the first time I am in a position to see it. I met you before addiction fully grasped you, I lived with you every day during your most active addiction, I was there when HIA was a speck of a dream and I've seen what God has turned it into. Being present gives me tremendous insight into the importance of the work of HIA but firsthand experience in the damage, destruction and desperation addiction causes both for the addict and those surrounding the addict. Going to the The Bridge furthered my knowledge in what leads each of us to use for the first time, whether it be drugs, alcohol, food, relationships or any other process addiction. All are a relief from the thoughts swirling in our heads that we are worthless, incapable, unloved, underserving and shunned. I understand each of feelings, I've done the work to accept why they are there and firmly believe I have the ability to come alongside the recovering and show them the attributes God specifically gave to them.

I want to be your partner in every sense of the word. I want to be a powerhouse couple for God and a tangible example of His mercy every day. I feel this is where God is calling our relationship and me.

With that being said, I want you to know first and foremost, I understand you are the boss. All decisions lay in your hands for final approval without question. I will give you the respect you so justly deserve. I also realize that all the staff is working toward a single goal and in order to best attain that goal all voices and input are valuable, important and necessary.

Only God has given me the courage and insight to put this down on paper. I realize that I don't have any say in what my role will be but after lots of dedicated prayer and thought this is where my heart is.

I read that email and I thought: *things will never be the same.*

And I was right. That email changed my world. It certainly changed Ally's world. Shoot, it would go on to change a whole lotta people's worlds! Hundreds of lives have been changed and families restored because Ally chose to take a risk, to say YES and to hit send.

It was not only confirmation that God had such bigger plans for this than I ever dreamed of, but it was also the confirmation that God was restoring all the years the locust ate, that He was making good out of such a rough situation.

We quickly met the very next day. She laid out all her plans, and they were amazing, right down to the fundraising.

Now, remember how I was talking about not living a comfortable life? At this time, Ally was a very successful wedding and event planner in Oklahoma City. She had a thriving business, but she chose to sacrifice everything that was comfortable in her life and take a step of faith and help us open that home.

Throughout that time working together, we began to fall back in love. Of course, I was never NOT in love! But our relationship began to be rekindled romantically, not just on the friendship level. She finally started getting those goo goo eyes again for this bald man!

On December 24, 2015, nine years or so from the moment we met, I got down on one knee and asked her to be my wife. She said *yes* and the rest is history.

REMEMBERING YEAR FIVE

I remember the day I celebrated my fifth anniversary of living clean. It felt crazy even to say. It didn't seem to be real. Here is a brief excerpt from something I wrote that day to share with HIA:

Over the past few weeks, I've been asking myself this question a lot: 'What do I want people to know about the past five years of my life?' It's a tough question. It's a loaded question. Each time I think about it tears begin to stream down my face. I've been so blessed. My life has not only been saved, but it's been remade.

God has taken the ugliest aspects of my life and my choices and he's turned them into an exquisite masterpiece of restoration.

I feel like the luckiest man alive. I'm marrying my best friend, my true partner, a woman I will never deserve.

Someone who oozes care, compassion and creativity—things I lack desperately. She is my perfect match and I'm blown away she said yes.

I lead an organization that is so far out in front of my abilities it's comical. God has taken my selfish little dream of living with other sober dudes and created a movement with unfathomable impact and potential.

I have two of the kindest, forgiving, and understanding children on the planet. Kids who have put up with their daddy sharing his crazy story all over kingdom come. But not just put up with it, but supported it!

I have two parents who double as my biggest cheerleader and my agent. I'm nothing without them. They stood just as proudly with me on day one as I kicked and screamed my way into detox as they have each and every time I've stood to tell my redemption story. They haven't ever said slow down, please don't say that or don't go there, why are you doing this? No, they've just encouraged and supported me with everything they have.

But back to that question: 'What do I want people to

know about the past five years of my life?'

I think this is it.

I want people to know these 3 things. Hope is real,
change is possible, and God is love.

Hope is so real. During my journey over the past ten years, almost everything I've hoped for has come true. Even in the midst of my disappointments, God has brought me hope and often showed me that I wasn't dreaming big enough yet. And despite that, the dreams and visions God planted inside of me, He has watered and brought to life. What was once only a small "hope" has now become a thriving organization helping hundreds of people every day.

Hope, when birthed inside the will of God, is the most powerful thing on this planet. It's these hopes that God uses to pull us to more fulfilled and free lives. It's these hopes that God uses to provide for the joys of our hearts.

Hope has pushed me to become a better man. It's made it possible for me to live fully known, because I now believed I am fully alive. Hope does that.

There are people who knew me ten years ago who would

never for a moment believe I could be the man I am today. Sometimes you get burned over and over again to the point where you think no one can change. I know people thought that about me. But today, I have a purpose. I have made and am continuing to make something of my life. I am changed in so many ways. I take care of my responsibilities. I love life. I have friends. I have meaning. I care for others. I forgive. My words have meaning. I'm honest. I work hard.

I am changed.

It's possible.

You can change. The one you love can change, your son, your daughter, your spouse can change.

Lasting change is possible. I know because it happened to me. God loved me so much that He gave me a way out. He loved me enough to let me hit the bottom. He loved me enough to watch me suffer, cry, scream in agony, fall deeply into depression and slip slowly into isolation. He loved me enough to put up with my baseless ego and pride. He loved me back to health in detox, softly whispering to my soul, subtly reminding me that He was there. He walked with me down the trails and to the cross that sat in the fields of that treatment center. He heard me as I cried out for forgiveness, and He promised to give me a hope and a future.

God loved me through the blackest of sin and the darkest of days. He didn't leave; He didn't judge… He just loved. And when I got back on my feet, vowing to do better, but failed again, He loved me still.

Do you know God loves you? Really, really loves you?

Hope is real, change is possible, and God is love.

But it isn't always easy.

TRAPPED IN THE LAND OF UNFORGIVENESS

I need to be honest with you: there was a period of my life, not so long ago, where each morning I woke up pissed off. As soon as I was awake, my first thoughts went straight to specific people who had wronged me. And for whatever reason, during this bitter season of my life, the list just kept growing.

Morning after morning, my first thoughts would be of the person who let me down repeatedly; the gossiper who just couldn't keep my name out of his mouth. The person who I trusted as honorable but turned out not to be.

Every day for far too long, these types of people consumed my first thoughts of the day.

I was angry, on the brink of building some hefty resentment, and trapped in the land of unforgiveness! This emotional state was destroying me and stifling any positive relationships I had in my life. And you know what? I was right where the enemy wanted me. I was stuck living in the land of unforgiveness; I was bitter, angry, and resentful.

Let me just be blunt with you. There is never any fruit produced when you live in the land of unforgiveness. You can't lead well. You can't "husband" well. You can't parent well. You can't even be yourself well.

A lack of forgiveness is like a root that grows into each area of your life, suffocating all it touches. It's like a poison you don't even realize you've drunk until it's too late and you've already started to succumb to it.

Lucky for me (and for you if you choose to apply this), I got a wake-up call. It came in the form of a random speaker at a church where I was telling my story. Funny how that works, huh? Before I spoke, this gentleman came onstage to share a bit of his story, speaking about how his father cheated on his mom while he was growing up, how his dad came out as gay when he was in high school, and then to top it off, disappeared from his life ten years previously.

He went on to describe how long he lived in the land of unforgiveness and where it took him. Not surprisingly he turned to substances and his life suffered for years. In describing his turnaround he said something I'll never forget: "I finally had to realize that if I wanted a life of freedom, I would have to live a life of forgiveness."

This simple statement shook me and changed me. In a moment's notice, I realized what I had allowed to happen and just how far away from God's purpose my stubborn cling to unforgiveness had taken me.

Maybe this is the wake-up call you needed. Maybe in this moment you realize how you've been waking up angry, frustrated and generally ungrateful. Maybe you, too, are trapped in the land of unforgiveness.

Want to leave that land and take your steps toward freedom? Forgive... because forgiveness is the essence of a life of freedom.

And you know what? God created us to live free! But when

sin entered the world, it created the land of unforgiveness and surrounded it with deep valleys filled with emotions like anger, rage, resentment, bitterness, and shame.

Thankfully, God so loved us and so longed for us to live free again He sent us bridge. It is a bridge back to the land of freedom. And that bridge is Jesus.

We now have the ability to take our steps back to the land of freedom!

Jesus took our sin on his skin so that we could live free.

His forgiveness of you sets *you* free, but *your* forgiveness of others allows you to *stay* free.

I hope I never return to that nasty land of unforgiveness. I know I am always just a few moments of weakness away. That's why I do what I do each morning to help me stay in the land of freedom.

M O R N I N G M A N D A T E

As I began to put some recognition around my time trapped in the land of unforgiveness, I began to see the importance of starting off my day with an overload of positivity, vision, and truth. Instead of dwelling in the depressed state of my mind, I had to begin putting words of victory into the atmosphere that would propel me toward the future I desired.

So, I started with something basic. As soon as my mind got fully revved up, I began telling myself each morning that today was going to be a good day.

I'd say it over and over and over again, and that worked for a bit, but I needed more. I figured maybe I should start telling others about the great day I was hoping to have. So I did. I began posting it each morning on Facebook: "Today is going to be a great day!!"

This worked really well for or a while. I loved the way it felt to share with others, as well as the positive feedback I almost always experienced. And it got tons of likes, which always feels good right?!

But by lunchtime, I was still struggling to stay positive. And that's when it hit me.

If I desired to live a more peace-filled life, I had to begin every day by casting a powerful vision of grace and peace.

If I desired to live a more forgiving life, I had to begin to forgive people—*out loud*—each morning.

If I desired to push through fear and overcome things that

had held me back, I had to begin speaking faith, courage, and confidence over myself each morning to get there.

The Bible talks about this in Romans 12:2: "Do not conform to the pattern of this world, but be transformed by the renewing of your mind."

My sinful mind *must* be transformed. I need a fresh touch from God first thing in the morning or there's no telling where I'll go.

So, with all this in mind, I sat down one day and wrote out exactly who I wanted to be each day. I call it my Morning Mandate:

(Breathe in slowly for ten seconds; blow out quickly. Do this five times.)

Today is going to be a great day!

Today God has given me *everything* I need to be exactly what *he* wants *me* to *be.*

Today I will love Ally with everything in me, always putting her first and prioritizing our relationship and our future above all.

Today I will bring positivity, hope, and encouragement to everyone I encounter. People will walk away from our time together changed, inspired, and motivated to chase their dreams.

Today, when I struggle—and I know that I will—I will persevere. When I can't seem to forgive someone who has wronged me, I will remind myself of how much Jesus has forgiven me. When I begin to think negatively, I will look up and be reminded that God has placed me in this moment, during this specific time in history to make a difference! To change the world! Any time wasted on negativity keeps me from fulfilling the mission he has given me.

Today when I feel all alone and that there is no one that is going through what I am going through, I will force myself to realize that there is *nothing*—no, not *anything*—I can experience on this earth that my savior has not already experienced.

Today I am a winner. Today I am a fighter. Today I will outwork my competition.

No challenge, No change!

And today I will overcome all my challenges. I will step into those moments that scare me. I will dream so big that only God can receive the glory for my accomplishments.

Today I will push myself in all areas of life. I will make great decisions because God has given me wisdom. I am financially prudent, I am an incredible vision-caster, and I am child of the Most High God. He has specifically created me to make an impact for the kingdom.

TODAY IS GOING TO BE A GREAT DAY!

Every morning I wake up, post on Facebook, "It's going to be a great day" (okay, maybe I don't do that part *every* day), get in the shower, and read this Morning Mandate *out loud*! I have it laminated and taped to my wall. It stares back at me like a prizefighter. I know that if I don't read it, believe it, and claim it over my life, I'll get knocked out every time.

My life is lived one day at a time and my Morning Mandate enables me to start each day with a positive step towards freedom, being all that I can be. What would you put in your Morning Mandate? Write it out, start saying it, and see how quickly God rushes to meet you there.

ONE DAY STARTS NOW

By this point, we were hitting our stride. Ally and I had been married for a year, Hope is Alive had opened its second women's home, and things were really beginning to take off exponentially.

And of course, things are not always smooth and on an upward trajectory. I am a positive person by nature. I have my Morning Mandate. I have my wife. I have my ever-growing relationship with Christ. I have lots of avenues of positivity in my world.

But honestly? Sometimes life hurts. During Year Six, in the midst of a flourishing non-profit, with huge and scary goals that will only get achieved in faith—and seeing those things get achieved, I learned this valuable lesson: even then, life can suck.

For the first time in my life, I began to have battles with really severe depression. There were moments where I lost the passion for what I did. These moments were followed by moments of sheer panic. Like, uncontrollable, knock-me-down, think-I'm-about-to-die panic. I knew those were only moments—they aren't my life—but man, did they feel real.

I had fear push me back into a place of apathy, hesitancy, and worry.

I was let down by people very close to me, who I had put so much trust in. I was hurt, and that hurt led to a real anger, and that anger compounded the doubt, and the doubt accelerated the depression, the depression grew to fear, the fear promoted the anxiety and panic... and that cycle kept happening more and more, gaining momentum each time.

I am a naturally confident person, but I had multiple moments—entire days—of thinking and believing I'm not cut out to do what I am doing. Wrestling with a whole group of "D" words: depression, disqualifying thoughts, deep fear, devastating doubts.

And if I'm being *completely* honest (as if there's any other way for me to be), those moments haven't all stayed in Year Six, either.

But I have discovered the truth about what was really

happening to me. Every single one of those moments, each emotion, all the misplaced feelings and crazy cycles of out-of-character reactions and fears, all the panic attacks, the worry and dread—all of it was rooted in *lies* the enemy was trying to get me to believe about myself, lies meant to steal away what God has given me.

The enemy was trying to steal back my hope!

The enemy was trying to steal back my purpose!

The enemy was trying to steal back my story!

The enemy was trying to steal back my future!

The enemy was trying to steal back my freedom!

But why would he do that?

It's because the devil absolutely *hates* me. He hates what I stand for, hates what I am leading, hates who I help, hates what my story represents. He hates that I am made in God's image. He hates that I'm a new creation. And that hate means he will do *anything* to take me out.

And just to make sure you know this: I'm nothing special! The enemy hates *you* too! He is also stopping at nothing to take *you* out.

So you know what I decided, and what I hope you'll decide,

too?

I decided then and there that *I will not believe another lie.*

My calling is too great, my marriage is too important, my future is too bright, my story is too sacred, and the people God has given me to lead are way too valuable for me to get trapped in another lie from the evil one.

And the same goes for *you.* Your calling is too great, your marriage is too important, your future is too bright, your story is too sacred, and the people God has called you to lead are way too valuable for you to get trapped in another lie from the evil one.

Those lies are pernicious and persistent, so it takes some wisdom to overcome them. And it all starts with recognizing the lie in the first place.

We all have those people in our lives who are always blaming someone or something else for their problems. Didn't get your work turned in on time for the big meeting? That was your computer's fault. Coming up a little short on bills this month? It's the fault of that store you like for having a good sale. Slacking off on your fitness regimen? It's Krispy Kreme's fault for building a store so close to your house.

For months and months in this season I limped through, I kept thinking that all the problems and issues I dealt with were other people's problems. The tough times were because of this person or that person, his fault, their fault, my wife's fault, my parents' faults... it was anyone but me.

I kept seeing my circumstances on a worldly level, meaning I had lost my spiritual vision. I was only looking in the realm of humans and then thinking that what *people* were doing had no significance in the spiritual realm. But that is just not true.

The enemy will use other people to deceive us.

The lies often originate with another person, through some offhand remark, casual glance, or some nonverbal communication that sticks in our minds. Then we believe the issue is with a human, distracting us from the realization that we're being duped!

The issue is not with a person (and that includes yourself, by the way)—the issue is spiritual. The enemy just uses the person to start the lie. And we know this because the Bible has already told us what's happening, in Ephesians 6:12, which says:

"For our struggle is not against flesh and blood, but against the rulers, against the authorities, against the powers of this dark world and against the spiritual forces of evil in the heavenly realms."

It's right there, in plain English, in black and white. The first lie I bought was that I was just dealing with people. But on top of that, when the enemy got me to buy into the lie that my problems were "people problems," then I would begin to think I had some power over changing them, that I could somehow control them. But every time I would try to change them in my own strength, the person would disappoint me again, hurt me again, fail me again, and so the cycle would start again: depression, anger, fear, panic... depression, anger, fear, panic... depression, anger, fear, panic... depression, anger, fear, panic...

It wasn't until I fully recognized that what has happening is that the enemy was manipulating me into thinking that "people problems" equaled "permanent problems."

Let's say that someone would make some sort of comment about, oh, my leadership style, or my relationships, or my beard. The lies from the enemy would hit my heart, my mind, my body and make me feel a certain way; those feelings would try to goad me to make choices that would alter my destiny.

Lies try to convince you that temporary feelings should

change your permanent destiny.

That's the power of the enemy's lies.

RECOGNIZE THE LIES

That's why we must learn to recognize the lies because this happens to us all the time. I'm guessing you can relate to my emotional cycle. These lies and feelings are unbelievably universal.

But recognition helps us neutralize the lies. We recognize that lies start with the smallest things.

We recognize that misplaced emotions can be tracked back to a small lie we believed was true.

We recognize that what people say about us doesn't always align with what God says about us, and that he should always have the last word.

We recognize that seasons of doubting God because he hasn't given us what we want don't take away the lifetime of him giving us exactly what we needed.

We recognize that someone disagreeing with us doesn't disqualify us.

We recognize that our past failures don't prohibit us from a victorious future.

We recognize that what seems like harmless gossip between friends is a way for the enemy to sneak back into our minds and fill it with hateful thoughts about another person.

We recognize that lies can cause negative thoughts about others, making us resentful, bitter, and hating on everyone and everything.

We recognize that the easy excuse we find to keep from doing the next right thing is a lie from the enemy to keep us from experiencing the freedom that God wants us to have on the other side of our action, on the other side of the steps we take toward that freedom.

We recognize that the world is not going to end if we don't get what we want; that feeling is just the way the enemy gets us to buy into the lie of selfishness.

We recognize the lie of the enemy when it comes to relationships, that God-honoring romantic relationships and marriages are abhorrent to the evil one and that he will do whatever it takes to build up resentment, to get you to back out, to fall into unhealthy parameters, to get your heart broken— anything to kill your relationship.

So we know we have a lot of areas where we need to recognize lies. But how can we do that? We must test our emotions. We have to recognize that everything evil, every emotion or feeling that is not of God, is from the enemy, because he is working 24/7 to destroy your life.

The Bible tells us that we must be alert. Check this out:

"Watch out! Don't let your hearts be dulled by carousing and drunkenness, and by the worries (or anxieties) of this life. Don't let that day catch you unaware, like a trap. For that day will come upon everyone living on the earth. Keep alert at all times. And pray that you might be strong enough to escape these coming horrors and stand before the Son of Man." (Luke 21:34-36, NLT)

What does this mean? It means the enemy wants to lull you to sleep and then place that lie right in front of you. The unaware version of you will snap that lie right on up and give it a good home. But the version of you who is on guard for lies will leave it right there, maybe put a couple of orange cones around it so that you'll remember to leave it alone the next time you encounter it.

You must always have your head on a swivel ready to recognize what's really going on and be aware that we are spiritual beings. Things aren't just happening. Always, remind yourself, again: my calling is too great, my marriage is too important, my future is too bright, my story is too sacred, and the people God has given me to lead are way too valuable to get trapped in another lie from the evil one.

PICK UP YOUR HOPE

What if I told you that you could have immeasurable power in your heart and your hands? Power to shut down negativity, the lies of the enemy, the thoughts of disqualification, the issues of secret sin, the trouble you have breaking free from toxic relationships? Would you want to know how to walk in that power? Would you do all you could to discover that power?

The thing is: you already have it available to you.

It's called *hope*.

You just have to pick it up.

Now, this is an area where you need to be careful, because the enemy will promise you hope, but his hope is always a false hope. When I was chin-deep in my addiction, I had all kinds of false hope—hope that my next fix would be the thing to pick me up. I had a false hope in a high that promised to cure all my ills, take away all my pain, give me the escape I needed... and every time it failed me.

It was false hope.

Today, I have a faithful hope. Today, my hope is one I can rely on, trust in, and look back at to see that it has pulled me through, time and again.

You can have this faithful hope, too. Scripture tells us about it in 1 Corinthians 10:13: "No temptation has overtaken you except what is common to mankind. And God is faithful; He will not let you be tempted beyond what you can bear. But when you are tempted, He will also provide a way out so that you can endure it."

God will give you a way out of the traps of the enemy. God will give you a faithful hope... but you have to pick it up. You have to actively grab it. It's not going to just happen. You have to ask for it, seek it out, study it and then make it a part of you.

When you start feeling you're not enough, when your past failures start creeping back into your brain as if another slip is inevitable, when you start to get down on yourself: recognize those for the lies they are and then *pick up your hope.* Reach out to someone you trust and tell them you need some hope.

Let them know you're struggling and let them speak hope into your life.

When someone you love does something to steal your joy and rob you of your passion, when someone tries to hold you down and keep you in a box: recognize those for the lies they are and then *pick up your hope.* Write down a list of affirmations and remind yourself that who the Son set free is *free indeed.* Remember who you really are: you are victorious, you are a beloved child of the King of Kings, and you were made for greatness in the Kingdom of God. What you've been through doesn't define you, it's only refined you into the person you are today.

When you start thinking negatively about someone God has put in authority over your life: recognize that for the lie it is and then *pick up your hope.* Go to them and say, "I need to talk; I need to get this off my chest. I know that if I hold onto this, I might do something I don't want to do."

When you start to feel like you're not good enough and that all the hard work you are putting in to live a God-honoring life isn't worth it and you should just go do your own thing: recognize that for the lie it is and then *pick up your hope.* Look back on all the places God has taken you. Reflect on your journey with Jesus and why you're doing what you are doing. Let that give you hope for who you might be if you finish what you've started.

How do you pick up your hope? I think you probably already know, but here are a few ways that work for me:

- *Prayer.* Pray off the top of your head, or get a book of prayers and read through it. There are also tons of pre-written prayers online for just about every circumstance.

- *Praise.* Make a Spotify playlist of good worship that gets your mind right. Use it as a touchstone to center yourself and pick up your hope.

- *Scripture.* I have plenty of key passages that help me get back to my true self, but you can also play scripture roulette—open your Bible to a random page and see what you find there. The Holy Spirit may just guide you to a fuller understanding of yourself and your faith.

- *Exercise.* Nothing grounds me quite like physical exercise. Solo exercise is a great way to let your mind roam; team sports are a great way to get your mind off something and back on terra firma.

- *Conversation.* Talk it out with someone you trust,

someone you know is going to listen more than they will speak, who will be a shoulder for you to lean on.

ONE DAY IS TODAY

The biggest lie the enemy tries to sell us is the lie that everything you want to be and everything you want to achieve is so far out in the future that you might as well keep living the same life you've been living. The adversary tells us there is no way for you to overcome all your pain, all your bad choices, all your debt, and all your busted relationships. He tries to sell you the lie that you might as well stay trapped in bondage because you will really never be set free.

I bought that lie for a long time. I paid a hefty price for it, too.

And then I picked up the faithful hope, the living hope of Jesus that gave me the truth: I am no longer a slave to the lies of the enemy.

I lived that "One day..." life.

One day I might be who I want.

One day after I go through all the punishment I deserve, I might get out of this.

One day I might overcome.

One day I might be capable.

One day I might live the right way.

And then I latched on to this truth: "One day…" is *today*.

The hope of Jesus living in us means we possess hope for *today*. He doesn't say one day, after all your steps are done and all your rights have been wronged, and then I will set you free. No, scripture tells us "now is the day of salvation." (2 Corinthians 6:2)

Today I am set free.

Today I know who I am.

Today I have the power to change.

Today I have the hope to make good choices.

Today I have a sound mind that is capable of choosing what's right for me.

Today I can choose what people I want in my life.

Today I have talents and skills God wants to use.

Today I can forgive those who have trespassed against me.

Today I have a story that will set people free.

Today I am God's resurrected creation.

Jesus has delivered us from the thinking that one day, after we accomplish all these things, *then* we might live free. No,

Jesus rose from the dead so that we have hope that is alive in us! Hope that screams in our faces *we are free today!*

All those "One day..." moments that played in our minds? That day is today. And we don't have to live a life of regret over missed opportunities, because the Bible says therefore there is no condemnation for those who live in Christ (Romans 8:1). That means that nothing you've done (or haven't done) is standing in the way of your freedom in Jesus.

You were made to live forgiven and set free, and anything outside of that is from the enemy. We do not serve a god of guilt or a god of shame. We do not serve a god of bondage, of addiction, of selfishness. We do not serve a god of resentment or anger.

None of those are the gospel. The gospel of grace is that when you put your life in Jesus' hands, then you are free! You are free *today*, and your "One day..." is *today.*

Today is your opportunity to start anew, to claim the life you were created to have, to take your first of many steps toward freedom. You don't have to wait for some future date, until you get a certain amount of money in the bank or the career you want. You don't have to wait until you've got every area of your life perfect (mainly because you never will).

You don't have to wait until your "One day..." arrives.

One day starts now.

What are you going to do with your One day today?

I know what I'm doing with mine.

FAITHFUL AS TZ

I had no idea how tough year seven was going to be. But in order for you to understand just how tough, you have to meet my friend TZ, because this is the year he came into the program at Hope is Alive.

Like a lot of folks, Zach Arismendez was shy early on, trying to find his way and his place in the program. And he was just the sweetest, gentlest, most soft-spoken guy—the kind of guy where you wonder how he was ever somebody who had lied or cheated or manipulated people. He made instant friends, and a lot of times when you're in community environments like ours, you end up picking up nicknames as a sign of love and respect. We already had a Zach in our program, but he was pretty short, so to differentiate between the two, one became Short Zach and the other became Tall Zach. And, since nicknames often morph and shorten, Tall Zach became TZ.

TZ worked really hard to get to one year of continuous sobriety, a huge milestone in our world that we celebrate with something we call Culture Night. We gather everyone from all the houses in an area on the first Sunday of the month and everyone who's celebrated a year of sobriety that month gets the opportunity to stand up and speak.

When TZ's opportunity came, he was excited and nervous, but he channeled all that into a very engaging talk. There was something about it that just stuck... this was a changed man, a man who carried a level of vulnerability and authenticity we don't always see.

As Ally and I drove home that night, we got a phone call from one of the residents in the home where TZ lived. We immediately knew something was wrong.

"TZ's not breathing!" he said. "We're trying CPR but he's not breathing!"

Instantly my heart dropped.

This was the moment I'd feared the most.

We rushed to the house to find an ambulance and police cars parked out front. They wouldn't let us inside as the EMTs worked to save TZ's life, but it was evident from the very serious mood that something wasn't right. As soon as they loaded TZ up on the ambulance, I called his parents to let them know what was going on and the hospital where they could meet us.

After about an hour at the hospital came the scene I'll never forget as long as I live. A doctor walked down the hallway toward us, accompanied by the hospital chaplain.

The chaplain never delivers good news.

We would find out later that TZ had an undiagnosed genetic heart defect that caused a random heart attack.

He was clean and sober when he died.

I don't think any of us was ready to handle the shock, the pain, the grief of that moment. TZ's parents, Dawn and Mike, were devastated, sobbing over the loss of their son. Ally and I, were raw and hollowed out over the sudden departure of a man we considered a friend. A beautiful light extinguished far, far too early.

This began a season where we saw more death and pain than we ever had before. It was the funeral for TZ. It was the funeral for another HIA resident, Brandon Gilbert. It was the funeral of my friend Joel Klein. It was a wave of grief that really brought home the reality of life—and death—that so many families of addicts deal with.

Being the person who has spoken at these funerals and pointed people back to God became a crystal clear reminder of the life and death aspect of the work God has called me to do.

And to be clear: this was also a year full of sobriety celebrations and dozens of marriages I got to officiate. The healthy graduates far outweighed the funerals.

But we still had the funerals. There's nothing more real than that.

TZ SOBRIETY SPRINT

Before his life was cut short, TZ had recently begun to enjoy running. It was a good place for him to be, and it's impossible for me to think of that and not also automatically think of Hebrews 12:1b, which says, "let us run with perseverance the race that is set before us."

And then one day, it clicked. God gave me a way to honor this young man who passed away clean, sober, and saved. We could hold a 5K fundraiser and call it the "TZ Memorial Sobriety Sprint."

So we did. And I'll never forget all the people who showed up to participate. Not just runners who were there to remember TZ, but also so many people who had lost their loved ones. We gave people a way to honor those they'd lost, and it's since become one of our most meaningful annual events.

The first year, TZ's family participated. They just walked the course, taking that final stretch hand-in-hand, celebrating TZ, and celebrating the way God often does what he does best: make good come from the toughest of situations. They reminisced about how grateful they were to have that year of sobriety with TZ, grateful to have him back in their lives, grateful for the new joyous memories they got to form.

I think if anything at all, I've learned that our job at Hope is Alive is not to change lives. That's God's job. Our job is to infuse hope into every possible situation, and to inspire people to know that God is still with them, no matter how tough the days get.

The thing about tough days—especially when you work in this field God chose to put me in—is that they are never behind you. Some seasons are tougher than others, and sometimes it feels like entire years can get dark (like the pandemic year of 2020 we all lived through). But even in the good times, we still have tough days. But those can be incubators of personal and spiritual growth if we let them.

We must continually realize we never arrive at the end of self-development. We can always grow and become better people, more giving spouses, more relatable friends, more empathetic customers. But to grow, you have to want more.

HIA is all about more. More structure, more accountability, more opportunities, more activities, more, more, and more. We are a program of more filled with people who want more, which is an innate, deep desire that carries well outside of Hope is Alive and into the real world.

You may never have gone through our program, but you might be a person who wants to grow, who wants more for yourself and for this world.

This is a very good thing to desire, it's the same thing God desires.

God wants *more* for you, too.

WHAT'S YOUR SELF-TALK?

So how can you get to that place of growth? First, you have to remember that no one has a bigger influence on you than... *you*!

Did you know that we each have somewhere between 50,000 and 70,000 thoughts each day? What are you thinking about yourself? What's your self-talk sound like? Are you speaking positively to yourself or are you dragging yourself?

Your thoughts will dictate your destiny. What you think about yourself will have a direct impact on where your life goes. Your future, your success, your friendships, the fruitfulness of your life all are fueled by your self-talk.

So what are you saying about you? What's your first thought each day? Your last thought?

This is why I start my day with my Morning Mandate. It helps me recalibrate and make sure I'm facing the day with a win, with affirmations that point to my future and that remind me where I desire to see myself in years to come.

Outside voices can end up diluting and destroying our self-talk. And yes, that includes media voices like music, movies, and television, but most importantly, it includes people. The negative voices of those around you steal your potential future. If you're around people who bring you down, who use horrible language, who gossip, who complain, then you're going to dilute your self-talk. That's why we must surround ourselves with positive, uplifting people… and be that kind of person for others.

But here's the question that can really hurt: are *you* the negative voice in your life? Take an honest assessment of the way you talk about yourself. I'm not saying you need to be a Pollyanna about the realities of the world, and I'm *definitely* not saying you need to be like an addict who rationalizes and justifies everything as someone else's fault. I'm saying that you need to be honest about yourself and ask: are you being too critical, too negative, and too harsh?

Here's a challenge for you: for the next week, practice an over-the-top, super-positive form of self-talk and see where it leads. How do you think you'll feel by the end of the week?

HOW'S YOUR BOUNCE BACK?

Another area where you can set yourself up for deeper growth is what I call your "bounce back." Like I said earlier, one thing we know about life is that storms will keep coming. Death, grief, uncertainty, divorce, job loss… these are just a few of the storms you may weather in the near or distant future. They're all storms I've lived through, and in them I discovered that to be the best version of me, I have to develop a strong ability to bounce back.

I demonstrated crazy determination and fight when it came to my addiction. Nothing was going to stop me from getting my next high. This is the strength of the addict. But often when it comes to working hard to change our lives, fighting through discouragement, taking accountability, and the like, we can lose our fight.

But until you develop a fight to be the best version of you, then you are destined to repeat the same sad cycle of life. You have to be someone who has bounce back in them. When one door closes, you don't worry about it: you bounce back, ready to watch a different door to fly open.

How is your bounce back? How do you respond to the tough times? Do you numb out? Do you run the other direction? Or do you bounce back?

World-changers embrace the storms of life, because they are fighters who have developed a strong bounce back, knowing that those storms can lead to opportunities for growth and positive change.

Here's the cool thing about this: you are not fighting on your own! God is fighting the biggest battles for you already! Just don't give up. Keep growing, keep going, keep getting back up, keep doing the next right thing, and keep bouncing back.

WHERE'S YOUR FOCUS?

One of the many things I've learned over the past ten years of sobriety is that world-changers can't do it all. That's tough for me, because my personality is that I do not like to say *no*. You already know how much I love the power of saying *yes*! But unfortunately, that means I have the tendency to have way too many irons in the fire.

But what I've learned following other leaders, reading books, listening to speakers, and going to tons of conferences is that people who are laser-focused on where they're going, who they want to be, and how they can get there tend to be the most successful at achieving those goals.

Don't get me wrong: *focus* is not the same thing as *work*. You can be busy with work, but if you're unfocused, all you're doing is driving aimlessly. No, you have to have an idea about where you want to go.

So where's your focus? What goals have you set for yourself lately? What steps do you have planned out to reach those goals? What are you saying *yes* to? What are you saying *no* to?

Staying laser-focused is a mix of *yes* and *no*. *Yes* to the work I have to do on myself and *no* to the things that aren't a priority. *Yes* to giving back and *no* to selfish things that add nothing substantive to my life. *Yes* to daily personal growth times and *no* to directionless "hang time".

It's all a matter of balance and discerning God's will for your life. You'll remember that I was working a lot of consulting jobs when I started HIA, and God asked me: "Did I call you to be comfortable?" Those gigs were good for money, but they were distracting from my laser focus. It wasn't until I said *no* to the distractions and *yes* to God's calling that God began to bless HIA exponentially.

But here's something I've learned over time: Your *yes* and your *no* change as you go through new seasons of life. What was a *yes* when you were young and single may no longer be a *yes* after you get married, have kids, or get more established in your career. As you get older, you may have to learn to say *no* to things that were a *yes* not that long ago.

It's all a matter of maintaining your focus. You have to step back and become focused on saying *yes* to the right things at this right time to help you achieve your goals. Because God's timing is better than yours. I am living proof that if you just wait, the right and *best* person or thing will come along.

HOW STRAIGHT ARE YOUR FEET?

I once knew a guy who had a terrible injury resulting in a broken leg. He had to get a really long, leg-length cast, and the recovery time was on a really stretched-out time table. He eventually got out of that cast, and you know what happened? He started walking funny.

You know why? Because, after all that time with his leg in the cast, his foot was no longer straight! He had to work with a physical therapist to straighten out his foot so that he could walk straight, with purpose.

The really interesting thing, though, is that *he didn't know he wasn't walking straight.* From his vantage point, he was doing just fine. It was only the outside viewpoint, the view from farther away that helped him understand how he was *really* walking.

So who do you have in your life that's helping you straighten your foot? Who is the person you're allowing in your life to tell you when you are not walking straight? Is there anyone in your life that has the breadth and permission to give you feedback, to hold you accountable, to correct you when you aren't walking straight so that you get back on the right path?

ARE YOU EMBRACING YOUR STORY?

Life leaves scars on us. Growing up, living, learning, loving… these things can and will leave scars. But the cool thing about scars is that they always have a story about them.

People have lived with scars, wounds, and stories for centuries. There's nothing new about having these little badges of a life lived. But what are you doing with them? Are you covering them up, or are you flaunting them so that others see them?

Your past owns you, until you begin to own it.

We don't begin to heal until we embrace our broken moments.

Paul showed us this in the Bible:

"Because of the extravagance of those revelations, and so I wouldn't get a big head, I was given the gift of a handicap to keep me in constant touch with my limitations. Satan's angel did his best to get me down; what he in fact did was push me to my knees. No danger then of walking around high and mighty! At first I didn't think of it as a gift, and begged God to remove it. Three times I did that, and then he told me, my grace is enough; it's all you need. My strength comes into its own in your weakness.

Once I heard that, I was glad to let it happen. I quit focusing on the handicap and began appreciating the gift. It was a case of Christ's strength moving in on my weakness. Now I take limitations in stride, and with good cheer, these limitations that cut me down to size—abuse, accidents, opposition, bad breaks. I just let Christ take over! And so the weaker I get, the stronger I become." (2 Corinthians 7:10, The Message Translation)

Embrace your brokenness, share your story, and let God's strength come into your weakness. Appreciate the gift that is your story, and show off your scars. I guarantee there are other people who will recognize them, because they carry the same ones.

HOW QUICKLY DO YOU FORGIVE?

Look, I'm not going to spend much time on this, because you already know that you need to forgive people. I started this chapter talking about the heaviness of death and grief, and let me tell you: dealing with all those funerals really drove home the fact that we must live in a state of quick forgiveness.

Not only is bitterness a killer of freedom and resentment a wreaker of havoc in your heart, but you also just can't know how short someone's time on this earth might be, or *your* time. It's so much healthier and happier to walk through life with an attitude of fast forgiveness.

HOW PREVALENT IS YOUR JOY?

We've already established that living the life of a world-changer is wrought with ups and downs, but the key to weathering that roller coaster ride is simple: live in joy.

Smile. Love. Give. Share.

It's really the only way to deal with setbacks and tough seasons. After all, that's what scripture tells us in James 1:2-4:

"Consider it pure joy, my brothers and sisters, whenever you face trials of many kinds, because you know that the testing of your faith produces perseverance. Let perseverance finish its work so that you may be mature and complete, not lacking anything."

If you look at it right, life itself is a joy. We've been given the gift of new life and the wonderful task of co-laboring with God to build his kingdom. Even when this life brings us the deep, exquisite pain of losing someone as heartfelt and faithful as TZ, how can we do anything but revel in Christ's joy?

REVEAL & RELEASE

Early on in my sobriety, I had moments when I felt God was revealing a vision of what Hope is Alive could be, and that our community of a handful of guys in one home, full of miracles and restoration, could be replicated and reproduced. I believe God gave me a vision that this could take place anywhere in the country, but it wasn't until year eight when that vision was fully realized.

After years of hopeful anticipation, this was the year of fulfillment. This was the year when we opened *eight* homes despite only having opened no more than three in any previous year. We expanded into areas as far reaching as North Carolina and Wichita, Kansas. In addition, we opened homes in Tulsa and Oklahoma City. It was a year with an outpouring of community support, of financial support, and excitement.

It was a year of overflow.

But there was a lot of time between the dream of opening several more homes and the actual reality of 8 homes during Year Eight.

STALKING CRAIG GROESCHEL

During that in-between time, I knew that one of our key strategic partners would be Life.Church, the largest church in America. This church just happens to be based here in Oklahoma City.

(Fun fact: before I was sober, I used to go to Life.Church on the weekends hung over. I would be high, sitting back, enjoying the light show and the music.)

I watched Life.Church grow over the years, and as I began to get clean and sober and start HIA, I realized that, not only could they be a really strategic partner, but also that this church was full of people like me who were struggling as well, and that there was a lot of people that we could help that were inside that church, and that church's credibility and influence could provide incredible momentum to Hope is Alive in our own growth as well.

So I began to drop in when I could. I'd been watching Craig Groeschel, the lead pastor there, for many years, and he'd already had an incredible influence in my life. I put this mission out in front of me: I'm going to get in front of Pastor Craig and convince him to come speak at an event for Hope is Alive.

I began to develop a plan. Listening to what he said from the pulpit, I noticed he talked a lot about working out. In some of his leadership podcasts, he mentioned that he often worked out later in the day and sometimes he would meet a buddy at the gym.

It just so happens one Monday afternoon I was at a gym in Oklahoma City and I saw him. Putting together what I already knew about him, that he was a man of rhythm and routine, I realized Pastor Craig would be at this gym here in Oklahoma City on Mondays at 4:30.

And that's when I began to not-so-casually stalk him.

Every Monday at 4:30, I made sure I was there and that I was wearing a Hope is Alive t-shirt. I also made sure that he saw me. Some days the vibe was so magnetic it gave me the momentum I needed to make eye contact. The connection gave me the courage to greet him, or at least make sure I was in his line of sight. He didn't know me yet, but he knew who I was.

Then came the day for which I had longed. As I walked into

the locker room, he was walking out. I said, "Pastor Craig, I can't tell you how influential and important you have been in my life, how your messages speak to the residents in our homes. I just want you to know that we're really grateful for Life.Church and we want to be partners with you. All our values are aligned..." I went through my whole presentation in something like fifteen seconds.

Without missing a beat, he said, "Great! How many houses do you have? What's your mortgage on them? How many residents are there? What's the toughest part about your job?" and more. He proceeded to drill me with about ten questions in a matter of seconds.

I'm glad that the pre-workout was flowing because I was able to rattle off all those answers without any hesitation. I was on my toes, and I believe my preparation for that encounter was pivotal, because what happened from that conversation forward was a series of events that allowed us to strategically partner with Life. Church, to the point where today we are Life.Church's number one local mission partner throughout the entire country. Over 600 people from Life.Church volunteer to help us every single month. They've become our largest church partner without a shadow of a doubt.

(And just to wrap up that story: yes, about two years later, Pastor Craig spoke at a Night of Hope event for Hope is Alive, where over 1500 people had their lives changed forever. It was an incredible evening. I guess the stalking paid off!)

Life.Church and Hope is Alive aren't the only things based in Oklahoma City that are growing. In fact, I'd say one of the many things I love about living in Oklahoma City is how much the city itself growing. This is a thriving place with lots of new developments. Seems like new buildings are popping up almost every other day these days, and I love to watch them morph over time. You see the signs, the construction, and the work. You drive by every day and a little more gets done each time you pass. I love that anticipation, even if I have no plan or desire to actually go into the new place once it opens.

It's the wait for the reveal where I thrive. That little place of anticipation in between the announcement and the actuality. It's the same thing with a pair of shoes I want, or a movie I can't wait to see, or a new album from one of my favorite artists. I dig that time between the reveal and the release.

I think I like that space because it's a place where patience and desire get tested and grow. It's something that's not just taking place in the market; it's taking place in my life—and yours—right now.

It's a place where faith grows, where your foundation is built, and, perhaps the hardest of all, where you find out what you really believe. This is the place where you develop your character and increase your integrity. And I like to take you through three steps that help define this space.

STEP ONE: REVEAL

Think back on your past for a moment, when whatever you're doing now with your life was just a gleam in your eye or a flicker in your brain. What did that future look like back then? Was there a time when something just clicked, and things opened up for a moment, and a hope for that future rushed in? A time when you thought, *I can do this!*

That was your reveal.

But the thing is: something has to get changed in order for a reveal to be brought into reality. Those buildings I love watching go up? That doesn't happen until another building is torn down or some fallow field is torn up to make room for that new place.

It's the same thing with us. We can't have the reveal of a new "building" without first having old things unearthed so God can pour a new foundation. Whether it's a new job, a new fitness regimen, a new outlook on life—something has to get uprooted to make a way for that new reveal to come to pass.

Maybe you're reading this and asking yourself, *Why has nothing been revealed to me*? I can't say for certain—who can know that but God?—but I'd be willing to offer this as a possible explanation: maybe you haven't yet fully died to yourself. Maybe you haven't given yourself over fully to have that old way uprooted to make room for the new, revealed way.

Only those who are ready for the reveal can receive it. Or let's look at the way Jesus talks about it in the Gospel of Matthew:

The disciples came up and asked, "Why do you tell stories?"

He replied, "You've been given insight into God's kingdom. You know how it works. Not everybody has this gift, this insight; it hasn't been given to them. Whenever someone has a ready heart for this, the insights and understandings flow freely. But if there is no readiness, any trace of receptivity soon disappears. That's why I tell stories: to create readiness, to nudge the people toward receptive insight. In their present state they can stare till doomsday and not see it, listen till they're blue in the face and not get it. I don't want Isaiah's forecast repeated all over again:

Your ears are open but you don't hear a thing.

Your eyes are awake but you don't see a thing.

The people are blockheads!

They stick their fingers in their ears

So they won't have to listen;

They screw their eyes shut

So they won't have to look,

So they won't have to deal with me face-to-face

And let me heal them.

"But you have God-blessed eyes—eyes that see! And God-blessed ears—ears that hear! A lot of people, prophets and humble believers among them, would have given anything to see what you are seeing, to hear what you are hearing, but never had the chance." (Matthew 13:10-17, The Message Translation)

STEP THREE: RELEASE

Okay, before you start flipping back through the book wondering if you're missing some pages, no, I haven't skipped a step. I just want to talk about this process in a particular order, and right now, we're talking about the release.

Have you ever been released from something before? Maybe Human Resources released you from a job unexpectedly, or maybe God released you from a ministry you were ready to leave. Or maybe you've spent some time in jail and felt the blessed wonder of being released.

The point being the word *release* can have a lot of meanings. So what does it mean to you?

What about when I use it like this: God has called us to live in *release*. We must be willing to release our purpose, our future and our passions.

Follow me carefully here: today I am living in full release. My life makes sense. I know where I am going and I have a plan. I know what I am good at and what I suck at. I know who I am and who I want to be. I am *released* to live out what was once revealed.

This is right where I want to be: living released by God to walk wherever the Holy Spirit takes me. I am released to live out my full potential. I am released to step fully into opportunities that only God can give.

Doesn't that sound great? I mean, who *doesn't* want to live in release? Especially when we've gotten a taste of a life God has revealed to us is possible.

But here's the thing: while we tend to want to go from reveal to release immediately, it just doesn't happen that way. We can't go from step one to step three. We have to do the work in between, that anticipatory place.

We have to go through step two.

STEP TWO: RECOVERY

Sorry to break it to you, but recovery is what lies between reveal and release.

Okay, now that I've laid all my cards on the table, let's look at all three of these steps in order:

1. *Reveal.* This is about death to self in order to make room for something bigger, different, and God-authored.

2. *Recovery.* This is the hardest stage, because it's where

the rubber meets the road when it comes to faith, patience, perseverance, and growth. It takes real work.

3. *Release.* This is the fulfillment of everything you worked for in the recovery stage, when you're living fully released in God's will.

I don't think I can overstate how difficult the recovery stage can be. It's tough, it's daunting, and it can be discouraging, but it's right where God wants you to be.

You have seen something that's captivated you—a vision, a dream, a possible future—it's been revealed. But you must build up a foundation; you must put in the hard work to reap the benefits of the release.

And hear me now: it can be really hard to do that recovery work as you meditate on your reveal. You'll get rejected. You'll go through hardships and tests. You'll have to face some of the hardest things you've ever had to face.

But it's all worth it.

You're never going to believe this, but it reminds me of a story in scripture...

That same day two of them were walking to the village

Emmaus, about seven miles out of Jerusalem. They were deep in conversation, going over all these things that had happened. In the middle of their talk and questions, Jesus came up and walked along with them. But they were not able to recognize who he was.

He asked, "What's this you're discussing so intently as you walk along?"

They just stood there, long-faced, like they had lost their best friend. Then one of them, his name was Cleopas, said, "Are you the only one in Jerusalem who hasn't heard what's happened during the last few days?"

He said, "What has happened?"

They said, "The things that happened to Jesus the Nazarene. He was a man of God, a prophet, dynamic in work and word, blessed by both God and all the people. Then our high priests and leaders betrayed him, got him sentenced to death, and crucified him. And we had our hopes up that he was the One, the One about to deliver Israel. And it is now the third day since it happened. But now some of our women have completely confused us. Early this morning they were at the tomb and couldn't find his body. They came back with the story that they had seen a vision of angels who said he was alive. Some of our friends went off to the tomb to check and found it empty just as the women said, but they didn't see Jesus."

Then he said to them, "So thick-headed! So slow-hearted! Why can't you simply believe all that the prophets said? Don't you see that these things had to happen, that the Messiah had to suffer and only then enter into his glory?" Then he started at the beginning, with the Books of Moses, and went on through all the Prophets, pointing out everything in the Scriptures that referred to him. (Luke 24:13-27, The Message Translation)

They missed it, just because they couldn't stay to wait a few hours! Their new world would be revealed if they could have just chilled out for a little bit!

Another way I like to think of these stages is like the last three days of Holy Week. You have Good Friday, the day Jesus died on the cross and God's plan for mankind was revealed (though we only know that now, in hindsight). Then you have Silent Saturday, the day when all hope seemed lost, when the disciples' faith was tested, when they all found out who they really were. And then, finally, Easter Sunday, when Christ's resurrection brings new life, new beginnings, and a new existence.

So, what can you do with that? If you're in that recovery stage, you can just rest in it, remembering God put you there. I don't mean *rest* in the sense of *slack off and get lazy* but more as *accept where you are and determine to get everything out of it that you can.*

Will it take time? Of course it will. Will it be hard work? Absolutely. Will it be worth it? More than you can know.

Paul says this in the Bible as he is writing back to a group of people who were in between the reveal and the release themselves:

"There has never been the slightest doubt in my mind that the God who started this great work in you would keep at it and bring it to a flourishing finish on the very day Christ Jesus appears." (Philippians 1:6, the Message Translation)

Don't quit before the miracle!

Don't stop because it's hard!

Don't make excuses because it tough!

Push yourselves, push your brothers and sisters in Christ,

and may God release to you opportunities that blow your mind!

You are capable, you are called, and you have credibility.

YEAR NINE
GOD'S GOT THIS

Year Nine was a year of drastic and exponential change, not just for Hope is Alive, as we opened seven more homes, but also for me personally. And for me, it started with a book I read while on a much-needed vacation.

The book was called *The Circle Maker* by Mark Batterson, and it changed my life. I turned the last page on that book and walked away my faith strengthened to a place it had never been before.

Even before I got to that last page, though, I began to make huge changes in my prayer life. I started making declarations over my life, and since then I have made huge decisions, taken steps of faith, and am believing that God will provide and answer my prayers.

And you know what... He already has!

The book begins with a story about a man named Honi, who

lived just outside Jerusalem in the time right before Jesus was born. The land was undergoing a drought, and he was a sage who still believed in prayer. So, with a crowd looking on, he drew a large circle on the ground and prayed a bold and confident (but still humble and reverent) prayer: that God would send rain. And to show his devotion both to God and to his prayer, Honi vowed not to leave the circle until the rain came.

The legend continues with the rain coming first as a sprinkle, then as a downpour, then as a calming shower, each time modulated by Honi's powerful and ongoing prayer dialogue with God.

This story and what followed in that book rocked my world. It shined a light on the fact that I was lacking in my prayer life and, really, my faith in general.

Unlike Honi, I had become satisfied with the answered prayers of 3 years ago, 4 years ago, and 7 years ago.

I had quit asking God to do the miraculous in my life. I was a long way from "I never called you to be comfortable."

I came away from that book with four life-changing realizations:

1. God is truly for me! This can sometimes be hard to

believe at all stages of life, but it's an unchanging truth. God is on your side!

2. Only God can provide the breakthrough that I need. Because work is such an integral part to faith, it can sometimes feel like my breakthroughs are dependent on me. Not so! It's all in God's hands.

3. God is not offended when I pray for big things. Why would he be? He's God! Nothing is too big or difficult for him!

4. Every good thing that's come to me has been the result of someone's prayers. I am only here on this earth because people prayed for me. I am not in this alone.

Okay, let's take a closer look at these, one by one.

GOD IS TRULY FOR ME.

This is really a life-changing and fresh perspective that we must all get our heads and hearts around. God is for us! God is for *you*. And when we can internalize that truth, then we can also understand what it means: that God wants for us the same good things we want for ourselves.

Psalm 37:4 tells us: if we delight ourselves in the God, then he will give us the desires of our hearts. It's easy to read that and think, *Okay, this thing I want is a thing God will give me if I just follow him.* And I think that could be valid! But what if we read it like this: *These desires I have? I have them because God gave them to me.*

God knows us so much better than we know ourselves. He created us! And not only did he create us, but he created us *the way he created us.* That means He knows what makes you smile, what makes you laugh, what inspires you, what motivates you and challenges you. That also means He knows what gets you down, what is causing you to struggle and where you need Him to step in.

God is on your team. Sometimes it may feel like you're fighting God, but you never are. He is pushing, pulling, guiding, and steering you to better days. That is who He is. That is what He does.

Knowing this totally opens up the way you pray. If you haven't internalized this truth, you'll pray small prayers rooted in worry and fear that God may not want you to have what you pray for. But once you grab this realization, you will pray unafraid. You'll pray huge prayers, prayers that will change your life.

ONLY GOD CAN PROVIDE THE BREAKTHROUGH I NEED.

For doers like me, this is a tough truth in which to soak. I am so ready to think that what I accomplish is evidence of my abilities, my skills, or my strategy. I think can you *see that? I did that.* I'm so quick to puff up my chest, turn on some Drake, and walk around like I really did something.

But the reality is, on my own, I fall short. I have not provided a solution to any problems, overcome any obstacles, or done anything good on my own—it's all been what God has done *through* me. When I believe the lies that I have done something, then it's only a very short walk to thinking that the breakthroughs I need today can be found through my own strength.

Duh, I can't provide a breakthrough. Only God can! And you know what? That's such a relief.

GOD IS NOT OFFENDED WHEN I PRAY FOR BIG THINGS.

So many times, our prayers fall incredibly short of what God can really do. God loves it when we pray big prayers, when we get to the end of ourselves and admit, "Okay, God, I really need you to take over on this one." We must remember God gave us these giant desires, and He can fulfill them I ways we cannot imagine. That's why we need to pray for the big things, the things we can't accomplish on our own, and the things that can only happen because of divine intervention.

After I got fired from that treatment center and I moved back into my parents' house, I spent a lot of time praying big prayers. Night after night after night, I prayed and prayed and prayed for what would become Hope is Alive. And it was through those prayers that the vision developed. Vision of what this organization could look like, how it could operate, what my role would be in the middle of it. I am where I am today—and hundreds of residents and graduates of HIA are where they are today—because of big prayers. What a testimony to God's faithfulness!

EVERY GOOD THING THAT'S COME TO ME IS A RESULT OF SOMEONE'S PRAYERS.

I've had people praying for me for *years*. My dad, my mom, my wife, Sue, Mike and Tonia... I could go on and on. These are people who prayed for me not just when I was in the depths of my addiction, but also when I was in treatment. They interceded when I was working the first job and when I was back at my parents' house. They were on their knees when I was launching Hope is Alive and when I was riding the wave of those first few months. They prayed when I had a vision for expanding the reach of this ministry... every step of the way, I've had people praying obstinate prayers for me.

I am only alive today because someone was bold enough to pray for me and God was kind enough to answer them.

These four realizations led to some major action on my part, and my faith is so much stronger.

1. I wasn't praying big enough, so I started.

2. I wasn't praying desperately enough, so I started.

3. I wasn't praying often enough, so I started.

4. I was quitting before the miracle, so I stopped.

God can do anything and part of the anything is God wants to do something big in your life. He wants to fulfill that impossible dream He has given you, something you thought you could achieve.

So many of us need God to move in a radical way. We need

God to do the impossible.

I believe He can and He will!

But we need to and must ask. God needs to see us humble, broken and desperate for Him to do what only He can.

Where do you need a breakthrough? Is it in your family relationships, your finances, your vision, your profession? Do you need a breakthrough in your heart, in your willingness, in your love for your spouse, in your relationship with God?

How can the way you pray help usher in that breakthrough? Are you like Honi, someone who is desperate in their petitions, humbled to know that only God can provide the breakthrough they need and focused enough not to quit praying before the miracle?

Oh, and there's one more aspect to this… and that's the way you praise. Do you praise God, no matter what? It's easy to praise God when you're seeing miracle after miracle, but do you praise God through the trials and storms?

Ooh, how about this one: do you praise God in the quiet moments when it seems like nothing is happening? Did I just step on your toes, because I sure stepped on mine! But even in those times, we must remember that God is never "off the clock". I like to do that by remembering Psalm 121:1-4:

"I lift up my eyes to the mountains—where does my help come from? My help comes from the Lord, the Maker of heaven and earth. He will not let your foot slip— he who watches over you will not slumber; indeed, he who watches over Israel will neither slumber nor sleep."

GOD'S GOT THIS

This chapter has about 3000 words; but honestly, it could all be summed up into just these three: "God's got this."

What a hopeful message! It's so hopeful; I'm going to type it again:

God's got this.

Let that phrase resonate in your spirit so you really feel it. Maybe even take a moment to close your eyes, place your hand over your heart, take a few deep breaths, and say it softly to yourself.

"God's got this!"

I first wrote the words that became this chapter towards the beginning of the coronavirus pandemic of 2020, and those were days of uncertainty, filled with major ups and downs.

I had times when I felt so filled with hope, with creative ideas flowing. I was using technology to connect with people in new ways, and I had some huge moments of listening to worship music and feeling the presence of God.

But I honestly had far more moments where debilitating fear overtook me, where overwhelming anxiety almost paralyzed me, and when doubt and confusion led me mentally to places I'm not proud to admit.

Thankfully, every time I got off track, God reminded me of that three-word truth: God's got this. This served as the reminder and hope I needed to pull me through. It recalibrated me, refocused me, and realigned me.

As we headed into 2020, our Word for the Year was "mature," because we all felt that we were about to enter a season of maturity. We had no idea the coronavirus pandemic was coming until it hit the American consciousness on March 11, 2020. That night Rudy Gobert of the Utah Jazz tested positive for COVID forcing a cancellation of their game against the Thunder, a game which was supposed to be played right here in Oklahoma City.

Everything changed from that moment forward. Priorities shifted and perspectives adjusted on what was important and what was not. People got sick. People struggled. People died. We endured quarantine and trauma, which led to an unbelievable explosion in mental health struggles like depression and anxiety and addictions.

In addition to personal plans (we'll talk more about those in the next chapter); Ally and I had a lot of plans for Hope is Alive that the pandemic halted. It became harder than ever to hope, to expect that something good was coming.

And, of course, I'm an outgoing person, a guy who needs plans and activity, so it was hard on me personally. I was supposed to run a marathon with the governor of Oklahoma. I was supposed to speak at lots of new and different places. My cup is full when I get to go out and spread the message of hope, so I had to just sit home with an empty cup, pivoting and thinking of new ways to help our residents maintain sobriety and keep Hope is Alive thriving.

Walking through that journey of quarantine those two or three months was really challenging, and put us in a place where we had to really recalibrate what our priorities were and really to rely on those three words: "God's got this."

During the pandemic, I was on a phone call with a mentor

and they told me the pandemic would be the first major trial I've been through in my life. And at first, I nodded in agreement, but when I reflected on my life, I realized he was wrong.

This was my first pandemic, but it wasn't my first problem.

This was probably the first major crisis for my generation as adults, but it wasn't my first personal crisis.

This might've been the first time I was stuck in my home, but it was most definitely not even *close* to the first time I was stuck in life.

I was reminded of the time when I was so addicted to prescription pain pills that I would wake up out of a dead sleep in the middle of the night, my body physically so hooked on those pills that I would be lying in a pool of my own sweat, sick as a dog, alternating between burning up and freezing, my legs kicking uncontrollably.

I was reminded of being so alone, so depressed, so tired of feeling like I had nothing to live for, waking up each day only to fall into the same cycle of insanity again and again.

I was reminded of all the times I convinced myself there would never be a day in my life where I wouldn't take those pills that I would have to take them the rest of my life, just to stay normal, just to survive.

Thinking back on how bad those days were, how sad and depressing they were, how completely devoid of hope they were, I chose to remember this unalterable fact:

I made it through that then. I'll make it through this now.

If I made it through those three long years of addiction, of taking 50 pills of a day, of desperation and hopeless situation after hopeless situation, of devastation to every relationship in my life, then I can make it through anything, even a global pandemic.

Because, God's got this.

Maybe you don't have a story like mine, but I know you have had moments in your life when you can look back and see a turnaround, a comeback. There had to be times when you could clearly see God pulling you through, working in your life to bring renewal and redemption. There must have been seasons when you were struggling financially, physically, personally and God intervened. Or perhaps it was your marriage or the loss of a job but Father God came to your rescue.

God got you through that. He'll get you through this.

Whatever you're facing right now, the hope to overcome it

lies in the story of your life. The hope is inside you. Where were you when God found you? Did He pull you through? Did he make a way? Did he give you a way out? Of course He did!

God's got this!

Hang on to the hope that what you've overcame in the past is the greatest indication that, with God's help, you'll overcome whatever situation you find yourself in today.

What you're dealing with is nothing new, and it is neither beyond God nor above God.

We serve a good God, one we can trust, one on which we can rely.

And that good God, He's got this.

I CAN DO DIFFICULT THINGS

Throughout this book, I've written a lot about praying big prayers and seeing God come through, about walking in victory and triumph. But there's one area of my life right now, in year ten, I'm still waiting. These giant prayers that Ally and I have prayed— prayers that have been on our lips for almost five years—have still not been answered as of the day I write this chapter in early April of 2021.

As long as Ally and I have been married, we've been trying to have children. Like many husbands and wives, we've longed to start a family, and we've long had a child-sized hole in our hearts, and in our home, and in our family. Over time, as we've been unable to conceive, we started visiting doctors and specialists and various other medical professionals to help us understand what's not clicking. Eventually, they advised to look into in vitro fertilization (IVF).

The thing with IVF is that it is not an easy journey. Aside from all the diverse public viewpoints on it, it is an incredible physical and financial sacrifice. We had no idea the toll it would take on Ally, the amount of stress it would add to her physical, mental, and emotional wellbeing. But we were willing to endure any path if there was the promise of a baby waiting for us at the end of it.

Our IVF journey began in Colorado on Valentine's Day 2020, where visited a specialist who was billed to us as the best in the country. It was a great visit, and we came back from that time excited and prepared to get started.

And then COVID hit.

We were stuck in quarantine. No traveling, no crossing state lines, no non-life-threatening medical procedures.

The doctor pulled it all, indefinitely.

We muddled through quarantine as best we could (as everyone did). We tried putting our focus on one another and on meeting the challenges of running a very hands-on, community-oriented ministry that might have trouble flourishing in a time when we couldn't meet together. And that whole time, I dealt with a lot of fear in the back of my mind on how we were going to be able to make it through this and what Ally would have to do endure.

Eventually the clinic resumed treatments so, in September of 2020, we started our IVF journey. As I write this, we've spent six months walking through what have been the most painful, trying, and difficult situation in our life together.

The theme of year ten has been that we can do difficult things, and it has lived up to that theme. I've injected over 100 shots into Ally's stomach, arms, and legs, filling her with medications and hormones. Apart from trying her physically, it's put a large stress and strain on our marriage.

Nevertheless, God is still faithful. As God's done in the past, so He is doing now. Every time we've shared publicly what's going on in our lives, not only have we been met with incredible grace and loving arms wide open, but we've also been met with people who have had similar struggles. It's kind of like how you don't think anybody has a yellow car until you buy a yellow car. Then everywhere you go, you see yellow cars. It's been the same with this. As we began to share our infertility struggles and journeys, everyone we talked to ultimately have a story of somebody they knew or loved that had gone through this journey. That's given us hope throughout this entire process.

At the end of 2020, we finally had our first transfer procedure, where they implant a fertilized egg. We were so excited. Everything we'd been working toward was all going to culminate in this moment, and we would finally be growing a baby.

The way the procedure works, you're literally pregnant for about ten days before you find out whether the embryo took or not, and while its ten days on the calendar, it feels like ten years as you're living out that long wait. You carefully, cautiously start dreaming about what life will be like for this child. You believe for what's going to be the rest of this little human being's life. And you trust that God has led you this far, has put this dream in your heart, and will fulfill it. You put your brand new little family in God's hands and wait on pins and needles for the good news that it's going to take.

Except...the procedure didn't take.

We were devastated, absolutely wrecked. I've had a lot of tough weeks in my life, and this was probably the toughest one yet. Even though we didn't carry this child very long, it was still our baby. Our hearts were broken, lying on the floor, crying out to God. We went through the stages of grief for a little life we barely knew.

It was almost unbearable, but for that theme phrase: we can do difficult things. One thing about tragedies like this is that the outcome tends to be binary. Either it drives you closer together or it drives you apart. We will forever be grateful to God for the closeness that he brought into our relationship as we healed. It brought us together in ways that we'd never imagined.

We would go on walks together and spend that time just journeying with God, trying to understand why this was happening. Why was He not allowing us to be pregnant? We never got a firm answer, but we do feel in our hearts that God was doing a new thing in our lives.

This is why we chose to go through the process again, even though it would mean more hormones, more injections, and another trip to Colorado. It would require another transfer, another wait. Ally had been so incredibly strong, so incredibly resilient to fight the hormone battles, the mental challenges, and the emotional swings. I cannot fathom the courage it took to stare this in the face.

As I write this, we don't know how it will go. We don't have a definite answer from God; we just have the distinct sense that He's doing something new, that one season of my life is coming to a close and another season is about to begin. That leaves me incredibly hopeful.

As I close out this book, I've had ten years to reflect on this journey of sobriety. I can now confidently say God always desires to do new things in us. These things will expand our faith and take us to the very edge of our faith. But that takes us being willing to say *yes,* to being willing to try difficult things.

That's where Ally and I are today. We don't know how this particular journey ends; we just know we trust God and we believe the testing of our faith produces steadfastness, that we may be perfect and complete.

Here's something I do know: God uses every single test to give a new testimony. It's cliché but true: there's nothing wasted in God's economy. We are believing that this is going to be the time we find two lines on that pregnancy test. We can't wait to experience that moment of joy, the entire process of carrying a child, the miracle of bringing a human being into this world, the incredible honor of shepherding their soul through this life, the life-altering responsibility of introducing them to their Savior.

So I'm here today, writing this chapter and believing Jeremiah 29:11. I believe God does indeed have plans for us that are filled with hope in the future, and that he is able to do exceedingly abundantly beyond all than we can ask or imagine. We are believing and trusting God, continuing to shepherd the flock of 200-plus residents and close to 50 staff members of Hope is Alive. We choose to do it joyfully, believing God will bring us the incredible blessing of a baby to share with the world. A living testament of what God can do.

And no matter what happens, the truth still remains: we can do difficult things.

HARD TIMES

The pandemic year was really hard for Ally and me, since we thrive so much on personal interaction with our Hope is Alive residents and staff. It was so hard to have put those things aside or settle for the Zoom version of them. It was difficult not to be there in person to hear their struggles and celebrate their victories, to have to walk through their lives with them virtually.

But we never lost our belief. HIA started because we believe, with everything in us, in the people in our program. And we believe in you, too! We believe in the power, the ability, and the future of *you*. We believe you can change your destiny and positively alter the trajectory of not just your life, but also the lives of your loved ones and those around you. We really have this audacious belief that you can change the world.

We believe that you're not in this world on accident. God knew what he was doing when he created you, called you, and empowered you to be a world-changer. You have a purpose, and that purpose is not just to make friends (though you will), and it's not to have fun (though you will). It's not to make money (though you do) or even to go to church (though I hope you do!).

God put you on this earth to help him finish the work He started.

But before you can do that, you have to recognize who you are and why you're here.

So who are you?

You are a beloved child of God who has been chosen for greatness.

You are a beloved child of God who has been called to change the world.

You are a beloved child of God who has been gifted beyond comprehension.

You are a beloved child of God who has what it takes.

You are a beloved child of God who is more than enough.

You can shake history, you can break generational curses. You are creative and innovative. You are a good parent. You are a good spouse.

You are built to change the world!

But there's a catch. People who are chosen for greatness are challenged in incredible ways. The good thing is this: overcoming those incredible challenges produces incredible results.

Every. Single. Time.

You've already read it in this book, but it bears repeating. This is one of my favorite phrases:

No challenge, no change.

Challenges always produce some type of change in us, but not all change is good. After all, quitting is a form of change... but that's obviously not the kind of change we are looking for.

Quitting is easy. Finishing is difficult. Finishing takes the tough work.

Finishing pushes us to places we've never experienced before. It deepens self-confidence, strength, and perseverance, and builds in our brain the "muscle memory" to overcome tougher challenges in the future.

Look at the way the apostle James put it in scripture:

"Consider it a sheer gift, friends, when tests and challenges come at you from all sides. You know that under pressure, your faith-life is forced into the open and shows its true colors. So don't try to get out of anything prematurely. Let it do its work so you become mature and well-developed, not deficient in any way." (James 1:2-4, The Message Translation)

James is telling us not to quit before the miracle. It's an encouragement to stay with something until you get everything you need out of it. Don't quit before you are well-developed and not deficient in any way.

Half-measures avail nothing, and true change takes place when you do the work all the way to completion.

You and me? We're finishers.

We can do difficult things.

THE MOMENTUM OF CHANGE

So how do we overcome challenging circumstances? How do we put aside the things that keep us from living our full potential? How do we gain the stamina not to tap out when things get tough?

If life has taught us anything, it is that desire alone isn't going to get the job done. It is not enough just to want to overcome. Neither is it enough to rely on willpower, a useful tool that is crucial to develop.

I've seen a lot of real life change, and the people who have changed for the better, who are living a sustained life of success and influence, who are positively impacting those around them and are flowing in their gifting and calling.

I call this the momentum of change, and I even created a formula for it. Look:

_____ + small wins + self-confidence = momentum of change

With each small win in your life, your confidence builds. This leads to greater self-confidence and ultimately the momentum you need to overcome the challenges you face. This produces a radically changed life.

I was only about a month into my sobriety when I first started telling my story in front of people as a public speaker. Even though I'd grown up as a pastor's kid, I had no idea what I was doing. I had very little self-confidence and zero experience, so to say I was nervous was an understatement.

It was made worse by all the sweat. Every time I raised my head up to look at the audience and got away from my notes, I would perspire, especially on my head—a bald head, which, as you may know, doesn't hide sweat well. So the whole crowd could see me sweating profusely, which only agitated my nerves and made me sweat more.

The more I thought about sweating, the less I thought about what I was supposed to be saying. That only served to make me sweat more.

It was a vicious, dripping cycle.

So you know what I did? I started practicing telling my story. I'd go to Lake Hefner and sit by myself in the car, start up the voice memo app on my phone, and pretend I was speaking to a crowd. I would do it over and over until I got it right. Then I'd pop in my earbuds and go for a walk or go work out while I listened to myself.

I did this repeatedly, and with each listening session I was giving myself a small win. My confidence grew, which helped me slowly build momentum in my public speaking. I got more and more comfortable being in front of people (and I brought a towel to with which to mop my head).

Anytime I was faced with an opportunity to share my story in a more challenging way, like on a bigger stage, or at a new church, or to 3000 attendees at a men's conference, I would go back to that routine. Those small "micro wins" would gave me the confidence I needed to walk on stage and share, with passion for what God had laid on my heart.

This is the product of momentum.

Maybe you've seen this in your life before. Maybe you had something that scared you, something that made you nervous, something you might have failed at before. But you practiced, and through repetitious small wins, you got enough self-confidence to overcome the thing that used to beat you.

I wish I could tell you that those two elements—small wins and self-confidence—were all you needed to make that formula work, but I would be lying if I did.

There is one key element that is the foundation that leads to wins, confidence, and ultimately the momentum of change.

It's what you tell yourself about yourself. Or self-talk.

Self-talk + small wins + self-confidence = momentum to change

If we could somehow open up your brain and look inside your thoughts, what would we see? If we could listen to the way you speak to yourself, what would we hear?

What you tell yourself is what you become, because no one has a bigger influence on you than you.

Everything good in your life begins with what you tell yourself.

To be honest, sometimes we don't even know how destructive our thoughts can be, and how giving room to mental negativity can change the trajectory of our lives. Destructive thinking only produces a negative mindset, which creates an emotional cascade from nervousness to anxiousness, which in turn creates negative momentum where we spiral into self-destructive behavior.

Confidence begins and ends with our thoughts and how we express them to ourselves.

When we tell ourselves that we can't do something or we don't have what it takes, saying things like:

- Life is too difficult.
- I'll never be able to achieve victory.
- I'll never fight my way out of debt.

- I'll never be a giving spouse.
- I'll never be the parent my child deserves.

We immediately begin to spiral into self-doubt and all these thoughts become a self-fulfilling prophecy.

You have before you two paths. One path will lead toward destruction and it is paved with negative thoughts, gossip, poor language, and the like. The other path leads toward momentum and is paved with positive self-talk, small wins, and self-confidence.

You can take your first steps on that second path by starting to believe that you can do difficult things.

MOUNTAIN MAN

Not too long ago, a group of guys invited me to tag along with them to climb the 14,000-foot Crestone Peak in Colorado's Sangre de Cristo Mountains. It wasn't supposed to be too bad — just a couple of days hiking in the Colorado summer. I'm a pretty fit guy, so I figured: piece of cake.

Until the night before we set out, when we sat in my friend Brian's kitchen and he gestured to the table we sat around.

"The top of the mountain is only about the size of this kitchen table," he said.

And there was something about that image that struck me, and the panic set in. From that point forward, I let negative thoughts have their way in my head. The emotional cascade was swift. I went from nervousness to anxiousness to crippling fear. What if I wouldn't make it? What if I fell? What if we got lost? What if I got injured? All the possible permutations of how it could go wrong made their way through my brain.

Then I actually saw the mountain, and somehow it all got worse.

Never underestimate your brain's ability to make negative thoughts even worse.

We set out on our climb early in the morning. Like, pre-sunrise early. Pitch-black-because-the-sun-isn't-coming-up-for-hours early. I was incredibly cold, so much so that my foot felt like it was frozen.

I was wandering on a bum leg in the dark, and the plan was supposedly to be 14,000 feet higher by the end of the day than where I was right now.

I was in a bad way. I couldn't walk properly, and the dark prevented us from accurately spying the route markers, manmade mounds of stone called cairns.

We were lost.

Oh, man, did I ever want to quit. It was all I could think about, and if I'd been by myself, I just might have done it.

Except...

There was one tiny ray of a thought shining in my head, doing its best to cast light through all the negativity:

I can do difficult things.

That was all it took. I began to focus on that little ember of hope, fanning it into a flame of determination to keep going.

About that time, we found the first cairn. It was a small win, but a win non-the-less.

By the time we found the next cairn, my body had started to warm up and my foot wasn't bugging me so much. Soon after that, the sun finally came up and my self-confidence began to build. I was starting to get some momentum.

Then we reached our first summit, at just over a thousand feet. I started to feel even better, and the rest of the day was triumph after triumph.

It took everything in me to make those first thousand feet, but once I did, I'd built enough momentum that the remaining

13,000 felt comparatively easy.

I was a changed man on my way back down that mountain. I started that climb in anxiety and fear and ended it in total confidence. I've carried my experience there with me ever since; God used it to impart to me an understanding of the power of my words to myself

I had to come to the end of myself and endure suffering in order to gain a new insight into this grace-filled power. (I don't think it's a coincidence that this all happened on a mountain range whose name is Spanish for "the blood of Christ").

I can do difficult things.

This powerful mantra made its way back to our camp and became the theme of our trip. Many of the other men on that trip have begun using it in their own homes to teach their children how to overcome situations. One of men is a football coach, and this is the way he's begun to end his team's practices.

I believe God gave me that phrase not just to conquer Crestone Peak, but also to prepare me for the IVF Ally and I would go through only a month later.

We can do difficult things.

Because God is for us and God is on our side. He has given

us hope for a brighter future, a God-breathed calling, and a healthy life.

APRIL 26, 2021: TEN YEARS LATER

I'm literally writing these words on April 26, 2021, the tenth anniversary of the day I took my last drink.

I'm overwhelmed with emotion today.

I think sometimes we best measure God's faithfulness by looking back on the markers in our lives. We talked about this at the beginning of the book, but as I sit here today, I can think back to every single year, and all the moments, big and small, that made a mark. This ten-year journey and all the steps towards freedom that I've taken that have led me to the place where I am now.

That's really what I hope you take from this book: that no matter what goal you're walking toward, whether it's sobriety, a business, a positive health change, a family, firm financial goals, or anything else, that it's all just steps. You get there by doing the small work, day in and day out, one step at a time.

I hope that this book has given you some applicable and tangible examples of how to take those steps towards freedom.

Sometimes that means you have to get honest with yourself just to take that first step.

Sometimes that means picking yourself back up when your world falls out from under you.

Sometimes that means launching out into the deep, even though you're exhausted.

Sometimes that means you're going to fail.

Sometimes that means you have to walk through a series of realizations about what's true versus what's a lie.

Sometimes that means you walk through depression.

Sometimes that means you have to learn to want the more for you that God wants.

Sometimes that means you have to do the hard work of recovery in between the reveal and the release.

Sometimes that means you have to put everything you have—every ounce of trust, faith, and hope—into God and really believe God's got this.

As I look back on the journey of my last ten years, one person has been with me on that journey every single day, either in my heart or by my side, and that's Ally. Outside of God, she is the most important thing in my life. She makes me a better man and gives me something for which to strive. I want her to be proud of me. In some ways, every single day of my sobriety has been a living amends to her for all I put her through before these ten years of sobriety. She's made every area of my life better and more beautiful.

Our marriage truly is a miracle.

No matter what steps of freedom you're taking, God really wants to do miracles in your life.

Perhaps the most unbelievable part of this ten-year journey is that God never gave up on the vision in our hearts—our deepest desire and our most personal prayer—for a family.

Friends, God is a God of miracles. Tomorrow, April 27, 2021, I'm going to celebrate ten years of sobriety with my closest friends and family members. It's going to be an amazing and special night, and Ally and I going to close it out by standing together on a stage and announcing, for the very first time, that we are pregnant.

New life has begun!

God is a God of miracles. God is a God of faithfulness. God is a God of hope.

And *Hope is Alive* in us.

CONNECT WITH LANCE

@LanceLang

Lance@LanceLang.com

ABOUT THE AUTHOR

Lance Lang has devoted his life to inspiring hope in those suffering from addiction, sharing his own journey from addiction to brokenness to freedom. From growing up as a pastor's son under the watchful eye of small-town America to leading a $30 million project management firm at the age of 25, pressure to perform and live up to others' expectations was a way of life for Lance. As the heaviness of these burdens grew, Lance turned to drugs and alcohol to keep up, creating a years-long cycle of abuse and addiction that destroyed his hope and left him in a reclusive, depressive state he thought would be his life forever.

But God had a different plan.

Lance's pull to sobriety is nothing short of a miracle. God pursued him and in a moment's notice changed everything in his life. Since getting clean & sober in April of 2011, Lance has gone on to inspire thousands of others to do the same.

In October of 2012, Lance founded Hope is Alive Ministries in Oklahoma City. Soon after, his wife Ally joined him and under their leadership, Hope is Alive has grown from one home and five residents to 21 homes with over 200 residents working hard to radically change their lives. HIA's success rate is unheard of, with over 85% of all graduates successfully living radically changed lives today.

The impact of Hope is Alive is being felt in thousands of homes and will be evident for generations to come.

Lance is also a sought after speaker and a non-profit consultant.

You can connect with Lance at www.LanceLang.com

ALSO AVAILABLE FROM LANCE

This book is the story of how my hope departed, how it was restored, and how I've kept it alive. I wrote it for drug addicts, alcoholics, gamblers, sex addicts, hurt people, prideful people, and angry people. I wrote it for the fear-ridden, the guilty, the insecure, the obsessed, the perpetually disappointed, and anyone else caught in the tornado of destruction that is addiction.

Dreams are universal. The hopes we all have for our future, the plans we all sketch out in our minds. And then, somewhere along the way, those dreams slip out of our grasp. Whether through some kind of pain or worry, some guilt or mistake, or just the dull routine of life getting in the way, we lose hope and start to slide into normality. But it doesn't have to be this way! Those dreams can fuel your world once more, you just have to discover the transformative power of hope.

Worry. Fear. Pain. You think something might be wrong with your loved one—your son or daughter, your husband or wife, your mom or dad—but you can't be sure. Can it just be a phase they're going through, or can it be something worse? Can it even be addiction? Finding Hope was written with you in mind. Starting from diagnosing whether your loved one has a problem with addiction and taking you all the way through treatment and beyond, Lance Lang has created this field manual to help both you and your loved one get the help you both need.

Get a daily dose of hope by subscribing to Lance's blog at www.LanceLang.com

HOPE IS ALIVE MINISTRIES

For over eight years, Hope is Alive (HIA) has focused on their mission, to "radically change the lives of drug addicts, alcoholics and those who love them".

HIA serves addicted men and women through a long-term, highly intentional, mentoring home model unlike any other in the country. Men and women leave our program equipped emotionally, professionally, spiritually, financially, with their families restored and a toolkit of life skills that enable them to live healthy and fulfilled lives.

HIA currently operates **TWENTY-ONE Mentoring Homes** across the nation. HIA Homes have changed the way addiction is treated and produced incredible results.

HIA serves the families of addicts through community-based support groups, called **Finding Hope**. These free groups are held bi-weekly and facilitate the powerful, life-changing curriculum developed by HIA Staff.

HIA currently operates **TWENTY-SEVEN Finding Hope** groups across the nation. Finding Hope has helped to educate and inspire hundreds of families to build health boundary systems and establish emotional health.

If you or someone you love is struggling with addiction, please stop by the HIA table at the conclusion of this lunch. We are here to help!

If you'd like to learn more about upcoming volunteer opportunities, please stop by our table on your way out. Our staff will be happy to chat with you and help get you signed up!

Learn more about the Hope is Alive Homes and Finding Hope Support Groups by visiting **www.HopeisAlive.net.**

C O N N E C T   W I T H   H I A I   www.HopeisAlive.net

 hopeisaliveok   Hope_is_Alive